# Complex Enterprise Architecture

## A New Adaptive Systems Approach

John D. McDowall

Apress®

*Complex Enterprise Architecture: A New Adaptive Systems Approach*

John D. McDowall
Warrenton, VA, USA

ISBN-13 (pbk): 978-1-4842-4305-3
https://doi.org/10.1007/978-1-4842-4306-0

ISBN-13 (electronic): 978-1-4842-4306-0

Library of Congress Control Number: 2019932796

Managing Director, Apress Media LLC: Welmoed Spahr
Acquisitions Editor: Susan McDermott
Development Editor: Laura Berendson
Coordinating Editor: Rita Fernando

Cover designed by eStudioCalamar

Cover image designed by Freepik (www.freepik.com)

Distributed to the book trade worldwide by Springer Science+Business Media New York, 233 Spring Street, 6th Floor, New York, NY 10013. Phone 1-800-SPRINGER, fax (201) 348-4505, e-mail orders-ny@springer-sbm.com, or visit www.springeronline.com. Apress Media, LLC is a California LLC and the sole member (owner) is Springer Science + Business Media Finance Inc (SSBM Finance Inc). SSBM Finance Inc is a **Delaware** corporation.

For information on translations, please e-mail rights@apress.com, or visit http://www.apress.com/rights-permissions.

Apress titles may be purchased in bulk for academic, corporate, or promotional use. eBook versions and licenses are also available for most titles. For more information, reference our Print and eBook Bulk Sales web page at http://www.apress.com/bulk-sales.

Any source code or other supplementary material referenced by the author in this book is available to readers on GitHub via the book's product page, located at www.apress.com/9781484243053. For more detailed information, please visit http://www.apress.com/source-code.

*To my father, who taught me to always use the right tool for the job.*

# Table of Contents

About the Author .................................................................... ix

About the Technical Reviewer ................................................ xi

Acknowledgments ................................................................. xiii

Introduction ..........................................................................xv

Chapter 1: Enterprise Architecture in Practice............................ 1

Enterprise Architecture Is Broken ................................................ 1

Origins of Architecture Frameworks ............................................ 3

Rethinking Enterprise Architecture ............................................. 7

    Enabling Agility.................................................................... 8

    Guiding the Enterprise ........................................................ 9

    Relation to System Architectures ...................................... 11

Summary............................................................................... 12

Chapter 2: An Overview of Complex Adaptive Systems............... 13

Complex Adaptive Systems....................................................... 13

    Examples of Complex Adaptive Systems........................... 14

    Sugarscape....................................................................... 16

    Economics and Enterprise Architecture ............................ 18

Adaptive Systems and Enterprise Architecture......................... 20

    Focus on Goals ................................................................ 21

    Rules and Constraints....................................................... 23

    Harnessing Emergent Behaviors ...................................... 30

Summary............................................................................... 33

## Chapter 3: Overview of the Enterprise Architecture Framework..........................35

About Models ...................................................................................................36

   A Simple Example..........................................................................................37

   Deciding What to Model..................................................................................38

Primary Objects .................................................................................................41

   Goals...........................................................................................................41

   Strategies ....................................................................................................44

   Actors .........................................................................................................45

   Processes ....................................................................................................46

   Data ...........................................................................................................47

Secondary Objects..............................................................................................49

   Systems.......................................................................................................49

   Behaviors.....................................................................................................50

   Environment .................................................................................................52

   Standards ....................................................................................................53

Summary...........................................................................................................55

## Chapter 4: Primary Objects ...................................................................... 57

Goals ...............................................................................................................58

   Enterprise Goals ...........................................................................................59

   Architecture Goals ........................................................................................61

Strategies..........................................................................................................64

Processes...........................................................................................................66

   Process Example ...........................................................................................67

   Required Processes........................................................................................70

Actors...............................................................................................................72

Data..................................................................................................................73

   Syntax and Semantics....................................................................................74

   Modeling Data ..............................................................................................75

Summary............................................................................................................78

**Chapter 5: Secondary Objects** ............................................................. **81**

Behaviors ............................................................................................ 82

    Capturing Behaviors ....................................................................... 84

    Documenting Behaviors .................................................................. 86

Environment ......................................................................................... 88

    Infrastructure Environment ............................................................... 89

    Organizational Environment ............................................................. 91

    System Environment ....................................................................... 92

Systems ............................................................................................... 93

    Monolithic Systems ......................................................................... 94

    Component Systems ........................................................................ 95

Standards ............................................................................................. 97

    De Jure Standards ......................................................................... 98

    De Facto Standards ........................................................................ 99

Summary .............................................................................................. 100

**Chapter 6: Modeling the Enterprise Architecture** ........................... **103**

Dynamic Enterprise Architecture ........................................................... 104

    Bounding by Detail ......................................................................... 105

    Bounding by Time ........................................................................... 109

Creating Models .................................................................................... 112

    Modeling Languages ....................................................................... 114

    Modeling Tools .............................................................................. 119

    Model Sizing ................................................................................. 120

Change Control ..................................................................................... 122

Summary .............................................................................................. 123

**Chapter 7: Measuring Effects** ......................................................... **127**

Testing ................................................................................................. 130

    Test-Driven Development ................................................................. 130

    Operational Testing ........................................................................ 132

Continuous Monitoring ................................................................................ 134

    Portfolio Management ........................................................................ 136

    Policy Compliance ............................................................................. 138

    Enterprise Capability ......................................................................... 139

    Data Flows ......................................................................................... 141

Reporting ................................................................................................. 143

Summary .................................................................................................. 144

**Appendix A: References** .................................................................... **147**

Enterprise Architecture Frameworks ....................................................... 147

Enterprise Architecture Practice .............................................................. 147

Modeling Languages ............................................................................... 148

Complex Systems/Emergent Behaviors .................................................... 148

Miscellaneous ......................................................................................... 149

**Index** ........................................................................................... **151**

# About the Author

**John D. McDowall** is a specialist in the architecture, design, integration, and testing of enterprise information and data analysis systems. He also conducts independent research in the fields of architecture and system engineering. John has over 20 years of experience, including his current position as the lead architect for a major system-of-systems effort within the US Department of Defense. Over the years, he has learned what does and does not work in enterprise architecture, and he has developed the approach in this book as a result of the lessons he has learned solving real-world problems. He thinks it will be applicable to many other enterprise architecture efforts.

After graduating from the United States Naval Academy, John spent 11 years on active duty in the Marine Corps in a variety of positions. Since leaving active duty, he has worked as a contractor doing IT systems development and integration for a variety of projects in the logistics, command and control (C2), and intelligence communities. During this time, he completed his PhD in Information Technology. In addition to his full-time job as a specialist and researcher, John is an adjunct professor in the Computer Science Department at George Mason University. Check out his blog at http://jmcdowall.org/.

# About the Technical Reviewer

**Dr. Susan Farley** has been a software and database developer for over 20 years and has published several papers on decision support systems. She received her BS in computer science and mathematics from the University of Georgia, her ME in modeling and simulation from Old Dominion University, and her PhD in Information Technology from George Mason University. She has created an extension to the Structured Query Language (SQL) that allows users to generate and query stochastic attributes and designed algorithms to optimize the simulations for those attributes. Dr. Farley lives in Virginia with her husband, daughter, and troublesome cat. She enjoys photography and teaching her daughter (and cat) how to get into mischief.

# Acknowledgments

First and foremost, I would like to thank Gerhard Beck, whose battle cry "Architecture is useless, fire all the architects!" was the inspiration for this book. He has been an invaluable sounding board for the ideas presented here.

I would also like to thank Dr. Susan Farley for agreeing to be the technical reviewer on this book. Her keen insight and attention to detail were essential to ensuring the material is presented clearly.

I would be remiss if I did not thank the staff at Apress Media, in particular my coordinating editor, Rita Fernando, who guided a first-time author through the writing and editing process with good-natured professionalism.

Finally, I would like to thank my wife, Michele, whose confidence and support made this book possible.

# Introduction

The formalization of information systems architecture began when John Zachman first published his architecture framework in 1987. Since then, a number of other architecture frameworks have been published, but most of them are direct descendants of the original Zachman Framework. As enterprises incorporated more information systems, managers recognized the need to coordinate development efforts across multiple systems, and system architecture frameworks were repurposed to serve as enterprise architecture frameworks.

The information systems landscape has evolved in significant ways since 1987. Where enterprises used to maintain a few centrally managed system development efforts, they now maintain dozens or hundreds of independent development efforts. The waterfall development model has given way to Agile and DevOps. And it is becoming increasingly apparent that system architecture frameworks are not delivering the value that enterprise architecture is supposed to provide.

This is not to imply that traditional architecture frameworks are obsolete or in need of a major revision. On the contrary, the point is that it is time to recognize that enterprise architecture is a different discipline from information systems architecture, and as such it calls for a different approach.

The purpose of enterprise architecture is not to design information systems but to help an organization reach defined business goals. Traditional architecture frameworks are designed to help create information systems, and they start from the assumption that one person can fully understand the complex interactions among all the elements that make up a modern enterprise.

This is a book about a different way of thinking about enterprise architecture and a different approach to modeling enterprise architectures. The field of complex systems engineering recognizes that even a moderately large collection of systems interacts in ways that no one person can fully understand or accurately predict. By treating the enterprise as a complex system, we can take advantage of the emergent behaviors that characterize complex systems and make those behaviors work for us.

# CHAPTER 1

# Enterprise Architecture in Practice

Enterprise architecture, as currently practiced, began when John Zachman published the article "A Framework for Information Systems Architecture" in 1987.[1] Since that time, the practice of systems development has changed significantly but enterprise architecture frameworks have not kept pace, and in many quarters enterprise architecture is perceived as a failure. In this book, I describe a new framework for enterprise architecture development, one that discards the previous focus on system implementation and concentrates on achieving the enterprise's goals.

## Enterprise Architecture Is Broken

At the time Zachman published the original description of his framework, the information systems landscape was a much simpler environment than most organizations face today. Information systems tended to be monolithic and custom coded, built to run on specific hardware, and built to perform particular tasks for the large enterprises that could afford such an investment. Over time, the costs of developing information systems came down, making it common for organizations to have many independent development projects. Computer hardware became a commodity, and the link between software and specific hardware weakened. Zachman's information systems architecture framework was updated and renamed the enterprise architecture framework, and managers began using that framework to coordinate systems development efforts across multiple organizations. In time, a number of other frameworks were developed and remain in

---

[1] J. A. Zachman, "A Framework for Information Systems Architecture," *IBM Systems Journal* 26, no. 3 (1987): pp. 276–92.

J. D. McDowall, *Complex Enterprise Architecture*, https://doi.org/10.1007/978-1-4842-4306-0_1

use today: The Open Group Architecture Framework (TOGAF), the Department of Defense Architecture Framework (DoDAF), and others. All of them were derived from or heavily influenced by the original Zachman Framework, and all approached the problem of enterprise architecture with the same top-down methodology: begin with a high-level abstraction and recursively decompose it into more concrete representations until there is enough detail to implement the intended systems. And for a time, it worked. But, more and more, large enterprises are coming to the realization that architecture frameworks originally designed to support developing individual information systems are not well suited to the task of enterprise architecture.

Because we have been using frameworks that are not suited to the task of enterprise architecture, there is a growing consensus in the business community that enterprise architecture has failed. Jason Bloomberg wrote the article "Is Enterprise Architecture Completely Broken?" in *Forbes* magazine in 2014, and came to the conclusion that it largely is. He asserted that the problem with enterprise architecture is that framework's focus is on documentation and not on business objectives.[2] In a 2017 LinkedIn post titled, "The Death of Enterprise Architecture?" MaryAnn Welke argued that enterprise architecture's focus on technology instead of solving business problems has tainted the practice.[3] She advocated for a rebranding of the discipline and a renewed focus on business needs.

The fact that enterprise architecture has failed, or is perceived that way, presents a serious problem for both business managers and system developers. For business managers, the lack of an enterprise architecture system forces them to make important decisions without critical information. For example, publicly traded corporations must comply with a wide array of regulations from the Securities and Exchange Commission as well as other federal and state agencies. If corporate management does not understand the functioning and interconnections of its various finance-related systems, how can it determine if the corporation is in compliance with applicable financial regulations? And if system developers are not working within a defined architecture framework, it is likely that teams working on different projects will arrive at different, incompatible solutions to similar problems. For example, when different systems use different authentication mechanisms, users are forced to keep track of

---

[2]Jason Bloomberg, "Is Enterprise Architecture Completely Broken?" *Forbes*, https://www.forbes.com/sites/jasonbloomberg/2014/07/11/is-enterprise-architecture-completely-broken/, last modified July 11, 2014.

[3]MaryAnn Welke, "The Death of Enterprise Architecture?" LinkedIn, https://www.linkedin.com/pulse/death-enterprise-architecture-maryann-welke/, July 28, 2017.

multiple usernames and passwords for the different systems; this leads to frustration and poor security practices such as keeping a list of login names and passwords for each system. Such lists are a fertile hunting ground for those trying to gain unauthorized access.

If enterprise architecture as currently practiced has failed but the original needs that spawned it persist, then something else must be devised—a new way of solving those problems. We must learn from past mistakes and adopt a new approach to enterprise architecture, and doing so requires a framework designed to serve the needs of today's complex enterprises. A modern enterprise architecture framework must focus on business goals and support the organizational agility that is vital to successful enterprises in the 21st century.

To understand how enterprise architecture got to its current state, it is instructive to review the history of the discipline. Knowing how the current enterprise architecture frameworks were developed and how they have evolved will help highlight the factors that led to the current state of affairs.

# Origins of Architecture Frameworks

Before delving into the history of architecture frameworks, it may be helpful to define *information systems architecture* to help distinguish it from *enterprise architecture.* There is no commonly accepted definition of information systems architecture; over 300 definitions have been documented[4] and many of those are highly technical definitions directed at the academic community. My practical definition of information systems architecture is: "The major components, functions, and interfaces of an information-processing capability that will be deployed and used as a single unit." (Keep in mind that this is architecture, not detailed design.) An information system architecture is the starting point for developing the detailed system design and its focus is limited to implementing that system. As you will read in the remainder of this chapter, the techniques used in information systems architecture do not scale and are not appropriate for developing a modern enterprise architecture.

---

[4]Hannu Jaakkola and Bernhard Thalheim, "Architecture-Driven Modelling Methodologies," in *Information Modelling and Knowledge Bases XXII, 20th European-Japanese Conference on Information Modelling and Knowledge Bases (EJC 2010)*, Amsterdam, NL: IOS Press, 2010, https://www.researchgate.net/publication/221014046_Architecture-Driven_Modelling_Methodologies, pp. 97–116.

It is hard to overstate the influence that the original Zachman Framework still exerts on the practice of enterprise architecture. Nearly every enterprise architecture framework in widespread use today is based on the Zachman Framework. Figure 1-1 shows the derivation of a number of architecture frameworks in common use today.

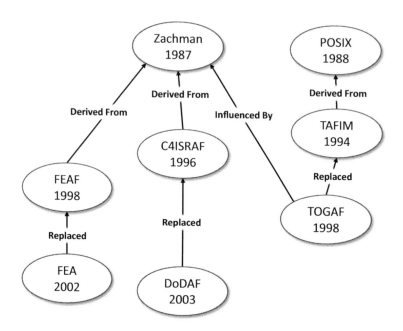

*Figure 1-1.* *Heritage of common architecture frameworks*

The Zachman Framework, first described in 1987, is still in use today. The Technical Architecture Framework for Information Management (TAFIM) was developed by the US Department of Defense (DoD) in 1994. The TAFIM framework was largely derived from the Portable Operating System Interface (POSIX) model (originally known as the IEEE P1003.1-1988 model). As its name implies, the POSIX model was originally developed to provide standards for operating systems in an effort to promote software compatibility across different versions of the Unix operating system. In 1998, the DoD ended support for TAFIM and it was taken over by The Open Group, where it evolved into the TOGAF model. In addition to its roots in TAFIM, TOGAF has been significantly influenced by the Zachman framework and is still under active development. During this same time period, the DoD developed the Command, Control, Communications, Computers, Intelligence, Surveillance, and Reconnaissance Architecture Framework (C4ISRAF). C4ISRAF, first released in 1996, was also derived from the Zachman Framework. C4ISRAF was replaced by DoDAF in 2003, and DoDAF remains the standard for information architecture development for US defense programs. Though not depicted, the UK's Ministry of Defense Architecture Framework (MoDAF) is closely aligned with DoDAF and derives from a similar heritage. Beginning in 1998, civilian agencies in the US government developed the Federal Enterprise Architecture Framework (FEAF), again drawing on the scaffold of the Zachman Framework. In 2002, FEAF was renamed the Federal Enterprise Architecture (FEA) and remains the architecture development standard for civilian US government programs.

As you can see, although the current enterprise architecture landscape appears to consist of a diverse array of competing frameworks, it is more accurately described as a family tree where all the members descend from the same root framework. To be sure, these frameworks have evolved in different directions over time. But the fundamental philosophy of top-down design that was established in 1987 with the Zachman Framework and article has not changed significantly in that time.

Today's systems development landscape is both more fractured and more connected than it was in 1987. It is more fractured in that there are few enterprise-wide system development efforts; for example, within a large enterprise, many suborganizations may operate independent system development efforts at vastly different scales. It is more connected because very few systems operate in isolation. Most systems have interfaces to other independently developed systems that serve different ends. Many information systems are deeply intertwined with physical systems, from simple pan-and-zoom controls in video-monitoring systems to complex cyberphysical systems such as modern fly-by-wire aircraft. The systems thus developed must interoperate with a dizzying array of commercial and custom systems that are each developed and upgraded on their own schedules. The result is an extraordinarily complex ecosystem that no one person, nor team, can fully understand.

Meanwhile, today's software development practices bear little resemblance to the development practices of the 1980s. Software systems were originally developed to operate on specific hardware, and updating the hardware meant updating the software. Software was originally developed using a waterfall methodology, where a lengthy requirements definition phase produced a detailed specification that software developers used to create the final product. Developers and system managers expected to deploy the software and move on to other projects; users would employ the system in that basic configuration until it was replaced. Updates to the system were handled on a case-by-case basis but followed the same pattern as the original system development: Design–build–test–deploy–move on to the next project.

Current software development practices have evolved significantly from that original model. With the exception of safety-critical embedded systems (e.g., aircraft flight control systems), most software is developed using the Agile methodology, where engineers flesh out the requirements and design details concurrently with the code development, producing usable products every two to four weeks and adjusting to new requirements as they go. Many Internet-based businesses, such as Facebook and Twitter, employ an even more dynamic software development methodology known as "development operations," or DevOps, where production systems are updated multiple times a day by independent teams each working on small elements of the systems. Development teams no longer build, field, and move on—they build, field, and continue to refine for years. Software systems are no longer fixed-code baselines; they are living things that are constantly evolving. Moreover, developers working in the 1980s and 1990s usually had to build the entire system from scratch because they were creating entirely new capabilities. Modern software is rarely built this way; most development efforts reuse large numbers of libraries and components that were developed by third parties. Today, software development is more about stitching together existing components than about creating new ones.

Such dynamism and complexity were not a part of systems architecture and development in 1987, when the foundations of most architecture frameworks were established. Furthermore, information systems are rarely developed in isolation any longer. Different information systems are being developed by different organizations and must interoperate when they are fielded, even if that interoperability was not foreseen by any of the development teams. The immediate needs of an enterprise may change faster than the system can be updated, or the enterprise itself may change its structure, resulting in a change in system requirements. These dramatic changes in systems development practice call for a rethinking of the discipline of enterprise architecture.

This is not to imply that the Zachman Framework, TOGAF, or other architecture frameworks are obsolete. On the contrary, the point is that it is time to recognize that enterprise architecture is a different discipline from information systems architecture, and, as such, it calls for a different approach. Where Zachman and others defined frameworks for designing an information system, this book lays out a framework to use in managing an enterprise that includes many systems, not only information systems but other types of systems as well. The enterprise architect has traditionally functioned as an information systems architect with enterprise-wide responsibilities, but this role must be transformed into that of a true enterprise architect, expanding beyond the focus on information systems to include focuses on business processes, enterprise strategy, and perhaps even organizational structure. This transformation requires an architecture framework that operates at a higher level of abstraction than the traditional information system architectures and is focused on different design aspects; a framework that can deal with the ever-increasing complexity of today's enterprises while avoiding the pitfalls that beset past approaches.

# Rethinking Enterprise Architecture

The information technology profession has borrowed the names of many roles from analogous positions in the building trades. Thus, we have "architects" who develop high-level designs that are turned over to "engineers" who develop detailed technical implementation plans. These detailed designs are turned over to the system "builders" for execution. Extending this analogy, the proper role of an enterprise architect is more analogous to that of a city planner: defining the goals of an organization, working with other senior managers to develop strategies to achieve those goals, specifying constraints for system developers, monitoring progress, and measuring results. Just as the city planner uses different methods and metrics than the building architect, the enterprise architect must use different methods and metrics than the system architect.

To define an appropriate enterprise architecture framework, we must understand the proper purpose of enterprise architecture. The purpose of enterprise architecture is not to design systems; it is to help an enterprise reach specific business goals. These goals may include raising brand awareness through more effective advertising, improving employee satisfaction through better benefits management, or whatever is important to the enterprise. Everything about an enterprise architecture effort should contribute to reaching the enterprise's goals; tasks that do not support the enterprise's goals are a waste of resources. It is imperative to understand that the systems that are ultimately built are not the end; they are only the means to an end. The end is achieving the enterprise's business goals, and that must be kept foremost in mind during any enterprise architecture effort.

Many business leaders have a distaste for enterprise architecture because they perceive it to be an effort focused on building models and diagrams that only make sense to the people who built them. It is important not to confuse enterprise architecture with modeling. Models are often useful, but too often enterprise architecture efforts degenerate into modeling for the sake of modeling. They become more focused on

of each system. By eliminating that level of instruction from the enterprise architecture, the enterprise architecture becomes a smaller, more focused, and more understandable effort. This focus enables the enterprise architect to concentrate on monitoring the enterprise's progress toward its goals and ensuring that the systems supporting those goals can interoperate and share data when needed.

This approach to enterprise architecture delegates detailed system design and documentation to the system implementation teams who are closer to the work and more familiar with the needs of the system's intended users. Delegating this work to the system implementers enables them to more rapidly adapt to changing conditions by eliminating the process of updating the enterprise architecture and obtaining the enterprise architect's approval before making changes. This approach is more suitable to today's agile development practices and reflects the way most system development efforts actually operate.

An enterprise architecture constrained in this way is a smaller and less complex affair than a traditional enterprise architecture. It does not attempt to specify implementation details of individual systems; it guides and constrains system design and development to ensure the system development effort aligns to and supports enterprise goals. In a large enterprise, this means the enterprise architect must give up a measure of control to enable organizational agility.

The reduced size of the enterprise architecture does not equate to reduced importance or a reduced need for precision in the architecture. On the contrary, the reduced size requires a more carefully defined and controlled enterprise architecture that managers can use to govern the enterprise. The architecture becomes one of the means used to guide the enterprise toward successfully accomplishing its goals. This transforms the enterprise architecture from a compilation of documents and diagrams into an operational tool that can be used to actively manage the enterprise.

Such an enterprise architecture requires fewer artifacts than other architecture frameworks, and it can be developed with simple modeling tools. Traditional enterprise architecture efforts that document all the implementation details of every system require complex models maintained in a dedicated tool by a team whose sole function is to maintain the model. This "priesthood" becomes central to all systems development because only a few select people understand the model, and all changes or additions require their involvement. This creates a bottleneck that slows development and limits enterprise agility. Reducing the scope of the enterprise architecture drastically cuts the number and complexity of the models needed to document the enterprise architecture. While this may not eliminate the modeling priesthood entirely, it removes it from the central role in defining the architecture and returns the enterprise's management to the role of focusing on the business goals, strategies for achieving them, and metrics for measuring progress.

# Relation to System Architectures

Attempting to decompose the enterprise architecture to include implementation detail expends effort on a task that is of minimal value at the enterprise level; that detail is only needed by implementation teams and not by enterprise management. The key to successful enterprise architecture is to document *what* a specific system contributes to achieving each business goal. But *how* that system contributes to the goal (i.e., the system's implementation detail) is beyond the scope of the enterprise architecture. In fact, system implementation detail should not even be directly visible from the enterprise level.

Solution architectures should explicitly derive from the enterprise architecture, but that derivation should be the only direct link between the enterprise and solution architectures. It is enough for the enterprise architecture to set up the definition that a system exists to support a given business strategy, the inputs and outputs of that system, and the effects that system has on the state of the enterprise (i.e., whether it performs any function that can be detected by an external observer). Any additional detail is extraneous and likely to be obsolete with each update to individual systems. Expending the effort to maintain more detailed mappings rarely yields any benefit worth the cost.

The remaining chapters of this book explain what an enterprise architecture should model, but not *how* it should be modeled (though I do provide some examples). How an enterprise should be modeled depends on the needs and goals of the particular enterprise. However, there is one important factor that must be considered, especially for large enterprises: The architecture must be documented as a formal model, meaning a mathematical representation that can be analyzed and assessed by computers. Diagramming tools such as Visio produce pretty pictures but they are pictures, not models. The use of a proper architecture tool such as Sparx Enterprise Architect, NoMagic's MagicDraw, or similar tools is imperative. I am tool-agnostic as a rule, provided the tool supports industry-standard modeling languages and data exchange formats (using nonstandard modeling languages and data exchange formats leads to vendor lock-in, always a risky proposition).

Avoiding the use of diagramming tools in favor of architecture tools does not mean that there is no visible representation of the model. Visual modeling languages such as the Systems Modeling Language (SysML) are built on a mathematical foundation that enables automated processing and assessment. This is vital to making the architecture more than just a dusty stack of papers on a shelf. By making the enterprise architecture a formal model, we can make use of automated-processing capabilities. Manually comparing diagrams and documents describing different systems to understand their relationships and gauge their conformance to enterprise guidelines is a difficult, time-consuming task. Using formal models makes it possible to use automated tools to compare solution architecture models to the enterprise model, and it will make it easier to compare the results of the enterprise's activities to the goals documented in the enterprise architecture. This transforms the enterprise architecture from an obscure pile of paper into a valuable, active management tool.

# Summary

Most enterprise architecture frameworks in use today derive from the Zachman Framework, an approach that was first described more than 30 years ago. Since that time, systems have become vastly more complex and interconnected and software development practice has evolved from a build-it-and-field-it paradigm to one where software is continuously updated during operations.

These changes in system complexity and development practices have exposed weaknesses in traditional enterprise architecture frameworks. The products of traditional frameworks are complex and unwieldy. Instead of serving as operational management tools, enterprise architectures often become bottlenecks that inhibit enterprise agility. As a result, many businesses believe that the discipline of enterprise architecture has failed.

Where traditional enterprise architecture frameworks focused on developing one or more systems, this book describes a new framework focused on achieving business goals, with system development relegated to its proper secondary role—as the means to an end and not an end in itself.

Adopting this new approach transforms the enterprise architecture from a static, document-centric consumer of resources into an active, operational management tool. Changing the focus of enterprise architecture from defining system details to achieving business goals places the enterprise architecture into its proper context as the means to helping achieve business goals.

# CHAPTER 2

# An Overview of Complex Adaptive Systems

A complex adaptive system is a system where each of the parts may be perfectly understood, but the behavior of the system as a whole cannot necessarily be predicted. The characteristics of such systems and their relevance to system design have been recognized for many years. Douglas Hofstadter, in his 1979 work on artificial intelligence, *Gödel, Escher, Bach: An Eternal Golden Braid*,[1] recognized the importance of the emergent behaviors that come from these systems. By the 1990s, commodity hardware powerful enough to efficiently run large-scale agent simulations was readily available, opening up a new avenue of research into complex adaptive systems. This research led to new insights in fields as diverse as economics and social sciences highlighting the effects of small changes on the behavior of large populations and how societies self-organize. We can use the insight that was developed from this research to improve the practice of enterprise architecture. Instead of imposing structure from the top down, we can let the structure emerge naturally from an environment bounded by relatively simple rules.

## Complex Adaptive Systems

Usually, the individual elements of a complex adaptive system are themselves relatively simple and operate according to a set of similarly simple rules. But when these simple elements are combined into a system, the system exhibits complex behaviors that are not readily predictable by examining the behaviors of the individual elements. That is, the system as a whole is greater than the sum of its parts and behaves differently than

---

[1]Douglas R. Hofstadter, *Gödel, Escher, Bach: An Eternal Golden Braid* (New York: Basic Books, 1979).

any of the parts. This phenomenon is known as *emergent behavior* and is one of the key characteristics of a complex adaptive system. To the outside observer, emergent behaviors may appear to be the result of sophisticated, centrally controlled optimization and prioritization of a system's actions. In reality, the emergent behaviors are the result of each of the individual elements of the system operating according to its own internal rules and motivations, in the context of the operating environment, and interacting with all the other elements of the system (each, in turn, operating according to its own internal rules and motivations). Put more simply, emergent behaviors are the result of each individual element of a system pursuing its own interest. It is these emergent behaviors that are of primary interest in modernizing the practice of enterprise architecture.

# Examples of Complex Adaptive Systems

One of the simplest examples of a complex adaptive system is a flock of birds. Anyone who watches a large flock of birds, such as starlings, in flight is struck by the way the entire flock moves as a coherent unit without any obvious leader. Moving from one place to another, turning in midflight, climbing, and diving all appear to be under the control of some director. The flock maneuvers as a unit to avoid threats such as predators and selects a landing place big enough to accommodate the entire flock, but there is no leader. This maneuvering of the flock is an emergent behavior of the flock as a whole. There is no leader making decisions and directing each bird. Each bird acts according to its own interests: avoiding collisions with other birds, eluding predators, and otherwise "looking out for number one." But when these individual birds come together, their individual behaviors combine to produce a flock that operates in the best interest of the species. When a single bird flying alone tries to elude a predator, the odds are in the predator's favor and over time the predators will kill many individual birds. But an entire flock maneuvering as a unit can confuse and intimidate a predator, dissuading the predator from attacking and thereby saving the lives of more members of the flock.

For a more detailed example, consider an ant colony. An ant colony is an example of something scientists call a "superorganism." A superorganism emerges when individuals of the same species become so highly specialized that they cannot survive without being part of a larger group composed of many individuals with complementary specializations. The group functions as though it were an individual, with each of its members being a small part of that individual. The behaviors of the superorganism are really the emergent behaviors of the complex adaptive system that is the group.

An ant colony displays a number of such emergent behaviors. The colony varies the number of ants that are sent out to forage for food; it maintains the nest; it cares for eggs and young ants; it fights off predators; and it completes many other complex tasks. For example, when one ant finds a food source, the ants will collectively find the shortest path to that source, a complex calculation for humans and one that no single ant is capable of. But an ant colony performs this task without any knowledge of mathematics, and, more importantly, without any central direction.

To better understand just how remarkable this phenomenon is, let's take a closer look at the composition of an ant colony. The exact composition varies depending upon the species, but most ant species have three types of ant: the queen, the soldier, and the worker. The queen ant establishes the colony, and after that her only task is to lay eggs. Despite her regal title, she does not rule the colony, nor does she direct the actions of any of the other ants in the colony. The soldier ants are relatively large ants with powerful mandibles. As their name suggests, their task is to defend the colony from threats such as predator attacks or other ant colonies infringing on their territory. Worker ants perform the routine tasks that keep the ant colony functioning, such as foraging for food and caring for the young. A closer examination of worker ants reveals some of the remarkable emergent behaviors of an ant colony, behaviors that no single worker ant is even aware of.

Worker ants leave the colony each day to forage for food. Foraging is a relatively costly activity: The colony must send out enough ants to find and retrieve the amount of food necessary to feed all the ants in the colony. Ants that are sent out to forage are not available to maintain the nest or care for young. Send out too many ants to forage and the health of the colony will suffer; send out too few to bring back enough food and the colony will also suffer. By the same token, time spent looking for and transporting food is time that cannot be spent on other tasks. The goal of the ant colony is not to find food. Rather, the goal of the colony is to maintain its own health and to propagate the species; finding food is just one of the tasks necessary to reach that goal.

Worker ants initially set out to forage for food without a specific destination, and each wanders the area until it finds a food source. Upon finding a food source, the ant returns to the colony. On this return journey, the ant releases pheromones, a chemical trail that helps other ants find the food source. The other worker ants in the colony have an instinctive inclination to follow this pheromone trail. This inclination is not an overwhelming drive and ants may choose other actions when presented with the pheromone trail; however, the inclination is strong enough that at least a few other ants will follow the trail. As other ants follow the pheromone trail and return to the nest with food, they reinforce the trail by releasing pheromones of their own, thereby reinforcing the inclination of other ants to follow the trail because stronger trails are more attractive.

It is possible that several ants will find the same food source at about the same time from different routes and each of the ants will return to the nest independently, leaving different pheromone trails. Other worker ants will then follow each of these pheromone trails to the food source and return to the nest, reinforcing that trail. Those ants that return most quickly will inspire more ants to follow their pheromone trail (it being fresher and stronger than other trails), and each of the ants that follow the first ones further reinforces the trail. Over time, the worker ants converge on the shortest routes and the longer trails are abandoned.

The result of all these individual actions is that the ant colony as a whole calculates the shortest path from the colony to the food source from among the many known paths—a task that no single ant could have accomplished on its own, and one that no central authority has directed. It is important to note that the ants have no instinct to find a shortest path. They have an instinct to find food, an instinct to bring food back to the nest, an instinct to follow a pheromone trail, and an environment that offers a network of many possible paths between the nest and any food source. With these simple building blocks, the ants perform a task that requires complex mathematical calculations for a human. It wasn't until 1959, when computer scientist Edsger W. Dijkstra published his algorithm for finding the shortest path between any two nodes in a network,[2] that humans had an efficient way to compute the shortest path between two points in a network.

# Sugarscape

Ant colonies are just one example of a complex adaptive system; we are surrounded with many examples of complex adaptive systems and our understanding of them is still developing. These systems remain an active area of research in fields as diverse as computer science, economics, and the social sciences. Agent-based software systems have been used in a number of research projects to observe emergent behaviors and study how small changes in the environment or the rules that govern the individual agents can have large effects on the resulting emergent behaviors. One of the seminal developments in this field of research is the Sugarscape model.

---

[2]E. W. Dijkstra, "A Note on Two Problems in Connexion with Graphs," *Numerische Mathematik* 1, no. 1 (December 1, 1959): pp. 269–271.

Sugarscape is a framework for growing artificial societies developed by computer scientists Joshua M. Epstein and Robert Axtell and described in their book *Growing Artificial Societies.*[3] Epstein and Axtell created an artificial environment and populated it with autonomous agents. They divided the environment into a grid and seeded select squares in the grid with "sugar," which served as food for the agents. They endowed each of the software agents with "vision" and the ability to "see" some number of squares as well as an internal reserve of sugar that could be replenished from any of the sugar deposits. They also gave each agent a set "metabolism," or rate at which it burns sugar. They programmed the agents to look around for deposits of sugar within their visual range, then move to one of the detected deposits based on a combination of the size of the sugar deposit, the distance to the deposit, and the agent's metabolic rate (i.e., how much sugar it would burn from its reserves to move to a given sugar deposit). Once at the deposit, agents consumed the sugar to replenish their internal stores. If an agent ran out of sugar, it died. Sugar deposits replenished themselves over time at a defined rate.

Epstein and Axtell observed the agents at work and were surprised at the behaviors that emerged from the system, even with only those simple rules. Where it would be natural to expect agents to converge on the largest sugar deposits, deplete them rapidly, and move on, the behaviors that emerged were more nuanced. Agents distributed themselves among the sugar deposits in a more efficient manner, with large deposits having relatively large numbers of agents but smaller deposits likewise attracting their share of agents. Over time, the environment would arrive at an equilibrium state (what ecologists call the "carrying capacity"). When environmental variations in sugar replenishment were introduced ("growing seasons"), patterns of migration that mimic what we see in nature emerged.

During the course of their research, Epstein and Axtell added more features to their agents, including the ability to reproduce, the ability to trade, and even the ability to modify their characteristics through cultural exchange. They observed things like the development of "tribes" of agents that emerged in different parts of the environment, with each tribe displaying distinct characteristics that had evolved over time. Economies also emerged among the agents, with surprising amounts of cooperation despite the agents existing in an environment where competition for resources was a specific design feature. A rough analog of human society emerged spontaneously from this group of simple agents.

---

[3]Joshua M. Epstein and Robert Axtell, *Growing Artificial Societies: Social Science from the Bottom Up* (Washington, DC: Brookings Institution Press, 1996).

The Sugarscape model demonstrated that even simple agents operating on limited instincts could combine and spontaneously generate sophisticated societies without any central organizing principle or force. It also demonstrated that even small variations in their environment could drive new behaviors. The results have been replicated in a number of subsequent studies and provide valuable insights not only into the production of agent-based software systems but also into fields such as economics, political science, and biology. Similar models are now used in many disciplines beyond computer science to better model the complex interactions of large, heterogeneous populations.

# Economics and Enterprise Architecture

Before the development of models such as Sugarscape, economic models were largely based on the assumption that the population is, in important respects, both homogeneous and rational. Homogeneous in the sense that all members of the population have the same goals (a higher income, lower prices, etc.) and rational in the sense that each individual's decisions are directed at maximizing their likelihood of achieving those goals. While these models are useful for understanding some aspects of societal behavior, they have significant limitations that are revealed when comparing predictions to observed behaviors.

Unfortunately for economists, reality often proves that traditional economic models are not accurate reflections of human behavior. The behavior of populations in the real world is very hard to predict. In addition, traditional economic modeling techniques are based on differential equations and partial differential equations, which make it difficult to analyze highly heterogeneous populations. In contrast, complex adaptive systems research gives economists a way to model and analyze both heterogeneity and the extent to which actors are not always rational.

Using techniques such as those demonstrated in the Sugarscape model, economists can create artificial societies that evolve over time, where individuals may alter their preferences based on experience and interactions with others. They can also increase the tendencies of some agents to act "irrationally" with respect to economic decisions. For example, instead of assuming that all agents in the model will act to maximize their own income, some agents may have a preference to remain neighbors with other agents, forgoing an increased income when presented with a choice between moving to increase income and staying put at the same income.

What does all this talk of economics have to do with enterprise architecture? Economics is fundamentally the study of interpersonal relations and how the aggregation of those relations results in business formation, growth, and evolution. Enterprises are composed of people, individuals who each have their own preferences, their own goals, and their own priorities. These characteristics affect how they perform their assigned tasks, whether they cooperate or compete with others in their own organization and other organizations within the enterprise, and their responsiveness to different incentives. All these individuals interacting with one another results in emergent behaviors of the enterprise as a whole—behaviors that may not be predicted and may not advance the enterprise's goals.

Traditional approaches to enterprise architecture take none of these aspects of the human element into account. Existing architecture frameworks assume that everyone involved is a rational actor and that each person and project will align to the enterprise architecture and act in the best interests of the enterprise. What usually happens in practice (i.e., an emergent behavior) is that implementation teams produce whatever documentation is required to satisfy the requirements specified by the enterprise architecture team, and once they receive approval to proceed, they focus on completing their assigned tasks on time and within budget. Communicating and cooperating with other teams working on different projects is a secondary priority. While the enterprise architecture may assume that one team will reuse components being developed by another team, the first team might be hesitant to trust that the second team will deliver the necessary components in time for the first team to meet its delivery schedule. As a result, the first team often just implements the needed component itself rather than worry about depending on the second team.

Ultimately, we see the same scenario play out over and over: Rather than relying on other teams to deliver critical dependencies on time, each project implements the needed functionality independently. This results in duplicated capabilities, often using incompatible interfaces that make eventual integration more difficult. Instead of the unified, interoperable ecosystem envisioned by the enterprise architects, the result is a fragmented, brittle conglomeration of systems with overlapping and inconsistent functionality. This requires a separate integration project, draining resources from the enterprise's main goals and requiring ever-increasing levels of effort to maintain and upgrade the resulting systems.

# Adaptive Systems and Enterprise Architecture

Every large organization is a complex adaptive system. Each individual is an independent actor driven by his or her own motivations, and those motivations may or may not align with the enterprise's overall objectives. While one developer may be driven by the prospect of career advancement, another may be driven by a passion to implement a particular technology even if it is not a good fit into the enterprise architecture. The architects of individual systems may tend to fall back on old techniques they are comfortable with, or they may be interested in trying the latest development techniques to see firsthand how well they work. This human element makes managing any large organization difficult. When combined with the ever-increasing complexity of modern systems development, it becomes nearly impossible to effectively manage an enterprise architecture using traditional techniques.

Traditional enterprise architecture frameworks do not take account of the human element and the resulting emergent behaviors of the organization. They assume that a complex enterprise can be constructed from the top down and that the development of individual systems can be managed using a command-and-control system that assumes near perfect visibility from the most abstract levels of the enterprise architecture to the most concrete implementation details. This necessitates a significant monitoring effort in order for the enterprise architects to ensure that individual system development efforts conform to the requirements of the enterprise architecture. Implementing this monitoring scheme requires design reviews, approval criteria, coordinating detailed schedules, and assorted other red tape focused on feeding the architecture, not on meeting the enterprise's goals. To a large extent, this monitoring effort is dedicated to countering the emergent behaviors of the organization and trying to drive development teams to adopt the desired behaviors instead of channeling their natural behaviors toward the enterprise's goals.

This does not mean that monitoring is unnecessary or undesirable; effective supervision is the key to success in any large endeavor. "Effective" is the key concept here—supervision does not need to be heavy-handed to be effective. Modern design and development tools make it easy to implement lightweight but effective supervision techniques. Automated test tools can ensure that systems conform to enterprise data-exchange standards, conformance-checking software can verify that system architectures are documented using the enterprise's selected language, and user feedback can gauge whether systems are meeting the needs they are intended to fulfill. When monitoring is automated, the implementation teams can check their own conformance periodically to ensure they are aligned with enterprise constraints. It is a form of test-driven development; a reliable form of self-monitoring.

The central insight of my approach is that the effort to drive behavioral conformance using techniques such as enterprise-level design reviews and detailed approval criteria is counterproductive. This does not mean design reviews and approval criteria are not important; they remain a critical part of the design and implementation of individual systems. But applying techniques that are appropriate for individual systems to entire enterprises makes the erroneous assumption that those techniques will scale up without adverse effects. These techniques do not scale well because of the sheer complexity of the enterprise as compared to individual systems. By applying these techniques at the wrong level, the traditional approach to enterprise architecture expends resources on ensuring conformance instead of on meeting the enterprise's real goals. Very few organizations have the development of a fully traceable, fully conformant enterprise architecture as their goal; the architecture is only a means for reaching that goal. By refocusing the enterprise architecture effort on meeting business goals instead of developing a detailed picture of the enterprise's systems, we can return enterprise architecture to its proper place as an operational management tool. As it is, enterprise architecture is relegated to the role of an esoteric technical pursuit that is only understandable to the modeling priesthood.

## Focus on Goals

*Never tell people how to do things. Tell them what to do and they will surprise you with their ingenuity.*

—George S. Patton[4]

System and enterprise architects generally come up from the ranks of engineers—system implementers who are trained to specify how a system should operate, build that system, and then test it to verify that it operates as designed. Engineers are not necessarily micromanagers, but they are used to understanding the inner workings of systems and tinkering with them to optimize their functionality. They tend to be skeptical of black box systems, preferring to understand the inner workings of the components they use. Engineers bring these habits with them when they become architects, and those habits

---

[4]George S. Patton, "Reflections and Suggestions," chap 1. in *War As I Knew It* (New York: Houghton Mifflin Company, 1947) p. 357.

often serve them well when building individual systems. But those habits do not serve the enterprise architect well. There are too many details in a large system of systems for any one person to understand, or even for a small group to understand. Enterprise architects need to give up their quest for detailed knowledge and their desire for control if they want to effectively manage a complex ecosystem.

General George Smith Patton Jr. was the preeminent American battlefield commander in the Second World War. His blunt language and strong opinions often made him a controversial figure, but both sides respected him as a brilliant operational commander and an inspirational leader. More than 70 years after his death, his leadership techniques are studied in military and civilian leadership development programs around the world.

Effective military organizations have long understood the benefits of ceding perfect knowledge in the name of organizational agility and mission accomplishment. Good military commanders accept the fact that detailed knowledge of their subordinates' activities is unattainable and unnecessary so long as the mission is being accomplished in accordance with their instructions. Instructions from commanders take the form of "mission-type orders." The commander specifies the desired end state (by saying something like, "Secure the perimeter of the embassy and protect those within it") as well as any restrictions or controls on the unit's activities (e.g., "Comply with the published rules of engagement"). The details of how the task will be accomplished are left to the subordinates who are actually performing it. There are several advantages of this approach. First, because the commander is not focused on the detailed planning for any individual task, he or she can focus on ensuring that the goals of each task align with the overall operational strategy. Second, the approach allows the subordinates tasked with implementation to respond to locally changing conditions without seeking approval from higher headquarters. This gives the on-scene personnel the flexibility to accomplish the mission quickly and efficiently. Another advantage of this approach is that it encourages innovative and novel solutions that are often more efficient than older ways of accomplishing the task.

Enterprise architects must be willing to adopt this goal-oriented approach to managing the enterprise's system development efforts if they wish to be successful in today's rapidly changing business-and-technology climate. The complexity of modern enterprises, especially those that are heavily dependent on large software systems, demands nothing less. No amount of documentation or wishful thinking will make up for the fact that there are only so many details one mind can comprehend. But the organization as a whole does comprehend all those details, and it is sufficient for the enterprise architect to leverage that knowledge. Unfortunately, directly using this kind of corporate knowledge is difficult because it requires knowing who has the specific knowledge needed to solve any given problem. Even in organizations where system design details are well documented, searching through the information to find the one or two pieces needed to address a specific problem is impractical. A better approach is to know which parts of the organization have that knowledge, and task them to solve that problem. Leave it those divisions to work out the details, and the enterprise architect can focus on observing the effects and measuring the results. That is, the enterprise architect leaves it to the enterprise's emergent behaviors to figure out how to achieve goals while he or she focuses on monitoring the results.

Establishing and modeling goals is discussed in detail in Chapter 3. For now, it is sufficient to understand that the enterprise must define its goals and monitor progress toward achieving them. By taking an adaptive systems approach to managing the enterprise architecture, the architect can make use of the latent organizational knowledge within the enterprise to achieve those goals. The key to effectively harnessing that knowledge is establishing rules and constraints that bound and guide the system implementation teams. Carefully defining these rules and constraints and keeping them to the minimum needed to meet the enterprise's goals provides maximum flexibility to the implementation teams, a key enabler of enterprise agility.

# Rules and Constraints

At its core, an architecture is a set of rules and constraints imposed on the system builders. The rules may include things like insisting that all system architectures be developed using a particular architecture framework, or that software must be designed using the Unified Modeling Language (UML). Constraints may take the form of requiring that systems use specific hardware architectures, such as requiring that all computer systems use an x86-compatible architecture in their central processing unit. Problems arise because people chafe at rules and constraints; it's human nature to rebel at having our choices limited. But rules and constraints must be enforced or they are meaningless. This is why most enterprise architecture efforts become focused on assessing the compliance of system architectures instead of achieving the enterprise's goals. And yet, we must constrain system builders' activities to ensure the enterprise's systems are compatible and can interoperate when needed. An effective enterprise architecture framework must balance the need to constrain system development with the need to focus on enterprise goals.

Before discussing the details of rules and constraints, we should define what they are and how they differ. Rules are guidelines that consist of more than hard-and-fast requirements. There are exceptions to every rule; the point of having the rule is to ensure that any exceptions are known and carefully considered. Constraints are more restrictive and generally do not tolerate exceptions; they are more akin to enterprise-wide requirements statements. While constraints may apply to the architecture or design of a system, they are usually applied to the system itself. Constraints are the primary means we use to assess whether the system fits into the enterprise architecture. Taken together, the rules and constraints of the enterprise architecture form the environment that system implementers must operate within. They form the "sugarscape" where emergent behaviors that are of interest to the enterprise architect will emerge.

# Rules

Within an enterprise architecture, rules are general statements about how the enterprise does the business of architecture. Assessing conformance to an architecture's rules may be more subjective that assessing conformance to constraints, but rules should be formulated to make that assessment as simple and unambiguous as possible. Rules are intended to govern the products rather than the behavior of architects and implementation teams; trying to govern their behavior would undermine our desire to take advantage of the emergent behaviors of the enterprise. Enterprise architecture rules fall into one of two categories: rules governing how systems are developed and rules governing how systems behave.

When establishing rules, the enterprise architect must take account of human nature and adapt the rules to those realities. People do not usually object to rules as such; people object to arbitrary, unenforceable, or unclear rules. We all have an innate desire to know how we measure up among our peers and whether we meet the standards expected of us within our field of endeavor. Clear, consistently enforced rules form the framework used to judge the degree of our success. The rules established by an enterprise architect for developing system architectures provide the framework for judging whether a system architecture meets the standards expected of it. As such, the rules should be relatively few and they should be clear and concise.

Rules can take one of two forms: they can define things that are prohibited or they can define things that are required. Within an enterprise architecture, defining rules based on what is prohibited is generally counterproductive. With few exceptions, it is hard to assess what a system architecture or implementation does not do. For example, the enterprise architecture could include a rule stating that no system may expose a network interface that does not employ Transport Layer Security (TLS) to encrypt data. But it would be simpler and easier to enforce if the architecture rules stated that all exposed interfaces must use TLS. For one thing, this is a clear statement. For another, the positive statement is much easier to test because of the inherent difficulty in proving a negative. There may be exceptions, but those exceptions must be clearly understood so the rules can be appropriately crafted. Rules that define prohibited activities or results must be unambiguous, so the implementation teams understand exactly what is expected of them in regard to those rules. In practice, you will find that it is much easier to craft clear rules defining what is required than crafting rules defining what is prohibited.

Rules that define what is required must also be clear and unambiguous. It is not sufficient to establish a rule stating, "All source code must be well documented." That is an ambiguous statement that is almost impossible to enforce. How do you define "well documented"? That is a subjective measure and it will require significant effort to assess conformance to it. Effort expended assessing conformance to a subjective rule is effort that could have been devoted to meeting the enterprise's goals. More importantly, this is an example of a rule that is inappropriate for an enterprise architecture because it attempts to define details of the development process that will only be visible to the implementation team; this rule has no effect on whether the resulting system contributes to achieving the enterprise's goals.

An example of a more appropriate rule would be: "System designs must be documented using UML 2." This is a clear, concise rule that is easy to assess. There are many tools on the market that can assess whether the system design is expressed in valid UML, so human interpretation is not required. It is also a rule that is easy to comply with, as design tools that generate valid UML are readily available. It is worth pointing out that this is a rule governing how systems are developed and documented, not how the system behaves. An example of a rule governing how a system behaves in relation to the rest of the enterprise would be: "All data within a system should be available through a public interface."

The important thing to remember when formulating rules is that people will inevitably find a way around them, especially when conforming to the rules is more work than getting around them. We can counter this tendency by ensuring that rules clearly contribute to some defined enterprise goal. This is necessary for both the enterprise architects and the implementation teams. The enterprise architects need to understand how the rule contributes to a specific enterprise goal or they cannot intelligently approve exceptions to the rule. Without that context for each rule, there is no way to judge the possible impact of the exception on the enterprise's ability to achieve that goal. The system implementers need to understand how each rule contributes to achieving an enterprise goal in order to intelligently apply the rule. People are less likely to try to work around rules when they understand the reasons for those rules.

Every proposed rule must be carefully considered to ensure it contributes to one or more enterprise goals and to ensure it will not have unintended adverse effects on system implementers. When we examine a proposed rule to understand how it contributes to achieving the enterprise's goals, we may find that the rule is actually counterproductive. For that same reason, we must periodically reexamine rules to ensure they are still helping achieve the enterprise's goals. Too often, rules persist over time and the original reason for the rule becomes irrelevant with the advance of technology or a change in enterprise goals.

It is important to keep rules as simple and easy to comply with as possible. The more burdensome a rule is, the more effort will be devoted to getting around it. When formulating a rule, it is important to consider how people will try to get around it and formulate the rule in such a way that avoiding it is either impossible or will take significantly more effort than complying with it.

It is also important to ensure that rules are stated as precisely as reasonably possible. The more ambiguous a rule is, the harder it will be to enforce. By choosing words carefully and ensuring that the meaning of the rule cannot be misinterpreted, we prevent the misunderstanding that results from the assumption that "everybody knows" what we mean by particular words or phrases.[5]

Finally, human nature should be taken into account. Sometimes, people will ensure they comply with the letter of a rule even if they don't comply with the rule's spirit, particularly when complying with only the letter of the rule is easier. So, think about ways people will try to "game the system" and formulate your rules with an eye toward preventing that behavior.

In addition, the rules should be kept few and simple, and it should be ensured that rules contribute to some defined enterprise goal. Whenever possible, it is useful to provide provenance for each rule. There is some reason the rule is in place, whether it is directly related to a specific enterprise goal or it is required by law or regulation.

---

[5]For an entertaining example of the miscommunication caused by ambiguity, see the old Abbot and Costello routine "Who's on First?"

Any rule that does not have a definable reason for being in place is arbitrary and a distraction from achieving the enterprise's goals. When people understand the reason for a rule, they will be more willing to conform to it. More importantly, everyone involved will understand when it is appropriate to break that rule.

There are some obvious exceptions to these guidelines for formulating rules. Rules derived from legal or regulatory requirements must be clearly stated, and everyone concerned must understand that violating those rules can leave individuals or the enterprise vulnerable to severe consequences. Such rules and their provenance must be clearly understood by all, and that means everyone must understand the consequences of failing to comply and the potential penalties.

## Constraints

Constraints are more concrete than rules. They are more directive and easier to enforce because they are easier to assess. Constraints are really enterprise-scale requirements and should be formulated in the same way as a good requirement. Constraints should be developed in conjunction with the tests that will be used to assess conformance to them, and those tests should be provided to implementation teams as early in the development process as possible. When the constraints and the tests are available to the implementation teams, it is easier for them to ensure that their systems will conform to the tests. Whenever possible, constraints should be assessed using automated test tools, allowing the enterprise architecture team to quickly and easily assess conformance. Most importantly, constraints must apply to the externally observable characteristics of the system because those are the things that contribute to achieving the enterprise's goals. Constraints that apply to the inner workings of a system are not only hard to assess; they remove the focus from achieving the enterprise's goals.

I use the term *constraints* instead of *requirements* because requirements are typically defined on a per-system basis, and constraints apply to the entire enterprise. More importantly, in some contexts the word requirement denotes specific legal and regulatory criteria that do not always apply to enterprise architecture efforts. For example, in developing systems for the US Department of Defense, requirements refer to criteria that have been approved through the Joint Requirements Oversight Council (JROC) process. Getting JROC approval for requirements can take more than a year and failing to meet JROC-approved requirements can be grounds for cancelling a program or for legal action against the contractor. In short, constraints don't carry quite the same weight as requirements.

Still, constraints should be expressed using the same type of language as used for requirements and their quality should be judged using the same criteria as those of requirements. That means they must be individually testable and enforceable. A common way to judge the quality of constraints is using the mnemonic SMART. A good constraint must be:

- *Specific*: A constraint must apply to a specific area that will be assessed.

- *Measurable*: A constraint must be measurable.

- *Assignable*: A constraint must specify what it will be applied to.

- *Realistic*: A constraint must be achievable with available resources.

- *Time-bound*: A constraint must specify when it will be assessed.

For a constraint to be specific, is has to apply to a defined, assessable part of the system. In most cases, this means that it applies to the external interfaces of the system where it interacts with humans or other systems. Making constraints as specific as possible ensures that test results are unambiguous. For example, a constraint like, "All systems must be secure" is not specific enough for a clear assessment. What specific aspects of the system must be secure? User authentication, network communications, data storage, and many other aspects of a system contribute to security and each of them must be assessed separately because each is secured using different means. A better way to express this constraint would be, "All systems must use secure communications protocols." This is still not a good constraint, but at least it is specific. We will improve it in the following paragraphs until we have a good constraint.

Just stating that systems must use secure communication protocols is not measurable. What defines "secure"? Unless we clearly define the term, we cannot measure whether the system is using a secure protocol. There are many network communication security protocols to choose from, some more secure than others. A better way to express the previous constraint would be, "All network communications must be secured using Transport Layer Security version 1.2 or later." This provides a clear, measurable expression of that we mean by "secure." Clearly, using TLS version 1.1 is not conformant, and it also does not apply to aspects such as strength of user passwords.

We still do not have a good constraint because it is not yet assignable. Systems have many means of communicating. They can invoke services across a network; they can send and receive e-mail—the list of means a system can use to communicate is extensive. Because this constraint has not been made assignable, it is not assessable; we do not know where on the system to perform the assessment. We can improve the constraint by restating it as, "All externally visible service interfaces must be secured using Transport Layer Security version 1.2 or later." We now have a good constraint, although it still needs to be judged against the "Realistic" and "Time-bound" criteria.

Determining whether a constraint is realistic should be as unambiguous as possible. We know that a constraint that specifies TLS version 1.2 is realistic because that protocol is in widespread use today and is supported by a wide array of programming languages and libraries. We could have specified some lower-level criteria, such as requiring that network interfaces use a 256-bit encryption key (which TLS does). This would still be a realistic constraint. However, specifying that network interfaces use quantum encryption would not be realistic because there are no commercially available quantum encryption devices on the market.

Finally, each constraint must be time-bound. When establishing constraints for an enterprise architecture, it is not necessary to place time bounds on every constraint individually. It is sufficient to specify time bounds in terms of the entire architecture. Because what we really care about is how the systems in the enterprise function when they are deployed, most constraints will be subject to assessment during final testing. They should also be subject to testing after they are fielded. Chapter 7 includes a discussion of the need to periodically test fielded systems' conformance to enterprise constraints. Systems evolve over time, and patches or configuration updates can alter their behavior. If we are to understand how systems contribute to achieving the enterprise's goals, we must be able to assess how they are contributing today, not how they were contributing when they were first fielded. And that means assessing systems periodically to ensure they still conform to enterprise constraints.

Just as rules should include provenance describing their reason, each constraint should include some statement of provenance. A constraint may be intended to enforce a rule, it may be intended to conform to an enterprise policy, or it may have some other reason. That reason must be clearly understood. A constraint that does not have a definable contribution to achieving the enterprise's goals is an indefensible drain on resources.

# Harnessing Emergent Behaviors

Once we have established the rules and constraints for the enterprise architecture and applied them to system development efforts, we have the ingredients needed to observe and take advantage of the emergent behaviors of the enterprise. The rules and constraints form the major boundaries of the environment that system implementers and users operate in—that is, they form the foundation of the enterprise architecture. How users and implementers respond to those boundaries and to each other results in emergent behaviors that will either help or hinder the enterprise in achieving its goals. Harnessing those emergent behaviors and channeling them toward achieving the enterprise's goals is the primary function of the enterprise architect.

All complex adaptive systems function within a framework of rules and constraints. An ant colony has rules; for example, worker ants must forage for food. An ant colony also functions with a number of constraints. Examples include there only being so much food that any single worker ant can carry back to the nest, there being a limited number of available worker ants, and so forth. Those rules and constraints can have dramatic effects on the resulting emergent behaviors. As the Sugarscape project demonstrates, altering rules and constraints changes the nature of the emergent behaviors. Giving agents the power to trade resulted in the emergence of trading networks and increased carrying capacity of the environment. Changing the metabolism of agents altered the distribution of agents and, in some cases, resulted in the emergence of migratory behavior.

The enterprise architect can likewise change the rules and constraints to affect the emergent behaviors of the enterprise. In this way, the enterprise architect can guide system development without getting involved in the details of how individual systems are designed or built. Ideally, the systems function as black boxes from the point of view of the enterprise architect: they take some set of inputs, produce some set of outputs, have one or more effects on the environment, and either do or do not conform to the constraints. That is all the information the enterprise architect needs about individual systems to guide the system development effort, and it provides half of the information needed to guide the enterprise toward its goals.[6]

---

[6]More detailed information may be necessary to perform other tasks that can fall to the enterprise architect, such as portfolio management. But this discussion is confined to the specific tasks of enterprise architecture.

The other half of the information needed is measurements of progress toward the enterprise's goals. This information quantifies the emergent behaviors of the enterprise. It does not explain those emergent behaviors, nor does it identify their specific causes. These are relatively unimportant processes in the field of enterprise architecture. Academics and researchers may have an interest in specific causes because they are trying to understand the science of adaptive systems. But the enterprise architect's interest is more practical: to achieve the enterprise's goals and to harness emergent behaviors toward that end. If the enterprise architect can identify correlations among specific rules and constraints with particular behaviors, that is a bonus. Just remember that correlation is not the same as causation.

Chapter 7 discusses enterprise monitoring in detail, but it is useful to touch on the subject here because monitoring is how we gauge progress toward the enterprise's goals. Enterprise goals are usually targets for the enterprise to achieve over the course of more than a year. Goals with a shorter timeline are difficult to achieve through any enterprise architecture effort because it takes time to adopt any enterprise architecture framework and see the results.

Armed with long-term goals and a means of measuring their achievement, and having reviewed the rules and constraints that system implementation teams must conform to, we can begin to monitor the results. These results are the outward manifestation of the emergent behaviors we want to harness. Measurements should be taken on a periodic basis to provide a means for establishing and understanding trends over time. Instantaneous monitoring (e.g., does a given system conform to a given constraint?) has its place, but because enterprise goals evolve over time, it is the behavior of the enterprise over time that is of primary importance to the enterprise architect.

Each enterprise goal will have associated metrics that are used to judge the enterprise's progress toward that goal. Several measurements will be needed to establish a baseline before any trends become visible. A minimum of three measurements is necessary, and those measurements must be spread across time to ensure the rules and constraints have had time to take effect. The time between measurements should be at least one month in an enterprise where systems are frequently updated, such as a DevOps environment. In an enterprise where systems are deployed less frequently, the measurement doesn't have to be done as often to provide meaningful results. Taking measurements every month tells us nothing about the rate of change if the enterprise only deploys system updates once per year.

Once a trend line is established, we can start to judge progress toward the enterprise's goals. If the trend lines are improving and getting closer to meeting the goals, we know we have an effective set of rules and constraints. They may not be optimal, but they are at least having a positive effect. If the trend lines are not improving, or are getting worse, then we know need to take action. The appropriate action is to review the rules and constraints and compare those to the observed results. The goal is to identify any correlations between the observed results and the applicable rules and constraints. It is important to remember that correlation is not the same as causation, but it does provide clues as to where to look for problems.

When correlations between observed results and one or more rules or constraints can be identified, it is the architect's task to ruthlessly examine the rules and constraints to determine if they are having unintended adverse effects. For example, it is possible that complying with a rule is having an different effect from the architect's intention. It is also quite possible that implementation teams' efforts to work around the rule are causing the adverse effects. Regardless of the proximate cause, the architect needs to change the rule. The rule can be discarded if complying with it is causing the unintended effect, or it can be reformulated to close loopholes if the problem is caused by implementation teams working around it. Another option would be to formulate one or more constraints that enforce compliance with the spirit of the rule.

After changing one or more rules or constraints, it will take at least two more measurement cycles to identify any trends resulting from the change. A single measurement will provide some hints about the effects of the changes, but at least two measurements are necessary to ensure there is a genuine trend emerging and not a brief anomaly in the data. This will also allow time for the changes to take effect in the enterprise and be reflected in the data; changes that have not yet had an effect on system implementation cannot show up in the data. More measurements over a longer timespan will yield a more accurate picture of the effects of the changes.

There may be times when the enterprise architect needs to change several rules and constraints at the same time. When making multiple changes, it is important to look at the changes as a whole and see if there are any predictable adverse interactions occurring. As any researcher will tell you, changing more than one variable at a time in any experiment makes it hard to predict what the results will be. What is important is to make changes, take the time to understand the state of the enterprise after those changes have taken effect, and repeat that cycle, continuing to refine rules and constraints as the enterprise evolves. This is a never-ending activity because enterprises and their goals evolve over time, and the behaviors that served an enterprise well in the past will not necessarily serve it well in the present or the future. The enterprise architect must continually monitor the enterprise and adapt to its changing needs.

# Summary

Complex adaptive systems are examples of the old adage that the whole is more than the sum of its parts. Surprisingly complex behaviors can emerge from very simple building blocks, and we can harness that phenomenon to improve the effectiveness of enterprise architecture efforts. Complex adaptive systems abound in nature, from ant colonies to flocks of birds. Researchers have developed frameworks to grow and study such systems under controlled conditions, giving us insight into how emergent behaviors can be affected by changes in environmental conditions even if we don't understand all the details of how those behaviors emerge.

Every enterprise, even a small one, is an adaptive system. But whereas small enterprises are relatively easy to govern, large enterprises produce many more emergent behaviors, which makes the enterprise architect's task particularly difficult. The desire to understand the details of each system's functioning and to ensure that system implementation teams conform to the enterprise architecture often results in a complicated system of design reviews and development policies. Many of these policies and procedures are directed at countering the natural emergent behaviors of the enterprise. This diverts attention away from meeting the enterprise's real goals. By applying the concepts of complex adaptive systems research to enterprise architecture, we can leverage the emergent behaviors of the enterprise to simplify the enterprise architecture and refocus resources on meeting the enterprise's real goals.

The enterprise architect's task is not to understand the details of how each system functions or to control implementation teams, but to channel emergent behaviors into productive activities that contribute to meeting the enterprise's goals. The key tools the enterprise architect uses to affect emergent behaviors are rules and constraints. By publishing clear rules and constraints that implementation teams will be reviewed against, the enterprise architect provides a clear definition of what must be done without directing how to do it. This gives the implementation teams room to exercise their creativity to ensure their systems conform to the enterprise rules and constraints while efficiently meeting their users' needs.

The resulting ecosystem of rules, constraints, and development teams will interact in ways that we cannot fully predict, leading to emergent behaviors that either improve the enterprise's performance relative to its goals or degrade that performance. Periodic assessments give the enterprise architect the data needed to identify and understand the enterprise's performance trends relative to its goals. This information can be used to update the rules and constraints to drive the resulting emergent behaviors in more positive directions, but it does require patience because behaviors do not emerge instantaneously, and so results can only be accurately measured over time.

Even if results are uniformly positive, it is important that the enterprise architect periodically reviews rules and constraints to ensure they are still aligned to the enterprise's goals. The business environment and technology change over time, and so the enterprise's goals will also change. The architecture must likewise change to remain relevant.

# CHAPTER 3

# Overview of the Enterprise Architecture Framework

An enterprise architecture framework is really a statement of philosophy. It spells out what is important about how enterprise systems should be designed and built and how they should interoperate with one another. Like any philosophy, it is a means of organizing one's thoughts about the task to be accomplished. The enterprise architecture framework is built on a foundation of model-based engineering. It relies on creating models that accurately capture the most important elements of the enterprise architecture in a format that enables automated analysis. It relies on carefully modeling what is needed to govern the enterprise and only those things; everything else is either completely extraneous or properly the domain of a solution architecture (i.e., an architecture for a specific system to be built).

In contrast to traditional enterprise architecture frameworks, I do not advocate a top-down recursive decomposition beginning with highly abstract constructs and continuing until there is enough detail to implement the necessary components and systems. Instead, I advocate creating one level of precise models that provides the guidance system implementers need to have to develop conformant systems that help the enterprise achieve its goals. For example, models of enterprise-level processes that support a specific goal or models of system interconnections that treat individual systems as black boxes. These enterprise-level models provide the foundation needed to assess the enterprise's progress toward its goals and to understand and adjust how the enterprise is operating. These models give the enterprise architect the data needed to perform automated analysis of the resulting systems and to understand the systems' contribution toward achieving the enterprise's goals.

© John D. McDowall 2019
J. D. McDowall, *Complex Enterprise Architecture*, https://doi.org/10.1007/978-1-4842-4306-0_3

# About Models

Before we delve into an overview of the architecture models, it will be helpful to define exactly what a model is. Many architects use the terms *model* and *diagram* interchangeably, but they are not synonymous terms. It is important to understand the difference between them and what makes a model more useful than a diagram.

A model is a specification of a system or part of a system using *formal methods*. That is all well and good, but what are formal methods? Formal methods are ways of using *mathematically precise* notation to describe something. A mathematically precise notation is one that has rules that define the syntax (structure) and semantics (meaning) of its symbols. Any equation from an elementary arithmetic text is an example of a mathematically precise notation. The syntax for an addition symbol is generally agreed upon (i.e., +), and its semantics are clearly defined (i.e., the number to the left of the + symbol should be increased by the amount of the number to its right). There are other semantics associated with the addition symbol, such as transitive and reciprocal properties. What is most important is that those semantics are defined and agreed upon. Everyone familiar with arithmetic who sees the + symbol shares a common understanding of its meaning.

In contrast, a diagram is a pictorial representation of something. Some diagrams may have formal syntax, but they are not mathematically precise. For example, anyone can use a drawing program such as Microsoft Visio to produce feature-rich graphical depictions of a system or an enterprise, but the semantics of the diagram are not well defined and are full of ambiguities. The icon that one user uses for a web server might be used by another user for a database server. The ambiguity can only be minimized by including a clear legend that specifies what each item used in the diagram stands for. Furthermore, the relationships among diagram elements are ambiguous. Many possible aspects of an element are not defined. For example, what elements may a web server be connected to and how may it be connected? Because this and other elements are not clearly specified, automated analysis of a diagram is a chancy proposition and will only yield accurate results within some range or probabilities. Diagrams are useful for conveying ideas to people, but their inherent lack of precision makes it difficult to subject them to automated analysis.

# A Simple Example

To illustrate the differences between a model and a diagram, consider the sine function familiar from basic trigonometry. We can define the sine function in three ways: using prose, using a diagram, or using a model. A prose definition of the sine function is, "For any acute angle in a right triangle, the sine is defined as the ratio of the length of the side opposite the angle to the length of the nonhypotenuse side adjacent to the angle." While this is correct on a technical level, it doesn't tell us much about what the sine function looks like or how it behaves. Furthermore, this definition is nearly impossible for a computer to understand and make any sense of.

Alternatively, we can define the sine function using a diagram. Figure 3-1 shows a graph of the sine function. Like the prose definition, this graph is technically correct. And it has the advantage of making it easier for people to understand how the function behaves. But the graph still doesn't provide a definition usable by a computer. Moreover, it is imprecise—different viewers can come up with different valid answers to the question "What is the value of Y when X = 1?" Answering that question requires reading the graph and interpolating among the values on the axes, an inherently imprecise activity. In addition, converting the prose into a graph or the graph into prose is challenging for a human and impossible for a computer.

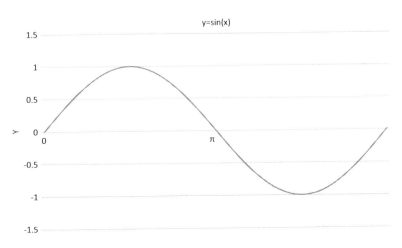

***Figure 3-1.*** *Diagram of the sine function*

Another way of defining the sine function is with a mathematically precise specification. Consider the following definition of the sine function: $y = sin(x)$. Any human conversant with knowledge of basic trigonometry will understand it. Any modern computer programming language understands this definition and can apply it. Every computer will resolve this function in the same way, and they will all return identical answers[1] to the question "What is the value of Y where X = 1?" And on top of that, this function will produce the graph shown in Figure 3-1 as needed. The prose definition is only needed for limited human uses and is readily available from a number of available reference works.

Many enterprise architecture efforts focus on producing diagrams because they are easy to produce and easier for senior executives to understand than formal models. Tools such as Gliffy, Balsamiq, Microsoft Visio, and many others can be used to create compelling diagrams. But it is important to understand that they are not models. They cannot be analyzed using automated means, and because their relationship to actual systems and interfaces is only as accurate as the diagram a person has produced, they must be manually updated every time the system is updated. Manually updating diagrams is time intensive and consumes resources that could be employed on tasks with more obvious benefits to the enterprise.

# Deciding What to Model

*All models are wrong but some are useful.*

—George Box, mathematician[2]

Do not let the previous discussion of formal methods frighten you. A wide variety of modeling tools are available on the market, and the main function of these tools is to make it easy for architects to create mathematically precise models simply and easily. These modeling tools provide an abstraction layer between the architect and the modeling formalism, using graphical notation instead of mathematics to describe the architecture. Stated plainly, they hide the details of the math and allow the architect to focus on the bigger picture. By and large, most of the modeling tools on the market have good support for common modeling languages such as UML, Systems Modeling Language (SysML), and others. This frees the architect to concentrate on *how* to model instead of *what* to model.

---

[1]They are considered identical although there may be rounding errors.

[2]George E. P. Box, "Robustness in the Strategy of Scientific Model Building," in *Robustness in Statistics* (Elsevier, 1979), pp. 201–236.

In a paper published in May 1979, the mathematician George Box observed that all models are wrong. [3] This is because every model, no matter how precise, is an abstraction of the thing it represents. An abstraction is wrong because it lacks some details of the original. If it did not lack those details, it would be a copy, not a model. When you undertake the task of modeling, you necessarily decide where the model will be wrong. But do not forget the second portion of Box's aphorism: some models are useful. The tricky thing in modeling is deciding what part of the model can be wrong while ensuring the model is still useful.

We speak of an enterprise architecture as a model of the enterprise, but that is not quite correct. In reality, an enterprise architecture is not a single monolithic model; it is a collection of related models. Each of those models is a description of some aspect of the enterprise, such as a particular information system. Some aspects of the enterprise are not modeled at all. That is, the architect has made a decision about which parts of the enterprise architecture will be wrong in that they are not depicted at all. It is the task of the enterprise architect to determine how much of the enterprise must be modeled for the architecture to be useful.

In addition to deciding which aspects of the enterprise to model, the architect must decide how detailed the models will be. For each of the models that make up the enterprise architecture, the architect must decide which parts must be captured precisely and which may be simplified or ignored. Again, the architect is deciding how wrong each model can be—which aspects of the model are most important and which can be safely represented by an abstraction.

There are no hard-and-fast rules to guide what to model and how detailed to make each model. Deciding what to model is an art more than a science, and that decision will vary as circumstances vary. For example, when developing a system model as part of the architecture of that system, the model must precisely define what the system will do and must represent exactly how the resulting system will function. But, as discussed earlier, an enterprise architecture does not need that level of detail; in an enterprise architecture such detail is waste of resources.

While there are no hard-and-fast rules when deciding what to model, there are some rules of thumb that can be applied. The most useful of these rules is that you should create models to answer one or more specific questions. That is, when there is some

---

[3]George Edward Pelham Box (1919–2013) was a British mathematician who made significant contributions to the fields of statistics, quality control, time-series analysis, and other fields. He founded the Department of Statistics at the University of Wisconsin-Madison.

aspect of the enterprise that the architect or managers need to understand better, it is probably a good idea to create a model of that aspect. The model should be detailed enough to answer the architect's or manager's questions but no more detailed than that. Any detail beyond that needed to answer these questions is wasted effort, and also increases the work required to maintain the model over time.

To illustrate this concept, consider a simple example. Assume that corporate management wants to know what kinds and amounts of data the corporation needs from external sources. Modeling the interfaces that the corporation's systems use to consume data from outside the corporation can help answer that question. But for this purpose, modeling the interfaces among systems within the corporation would be extraneous work—data exchanged among systems within the company is outside the scope of the question. There may be other good reasons to model those internal interfaces (and, as you will see later, there are very good reasons to model them), but it is important to understand that modeling internal interfaces will not help answer the original question.

Another good rule of thumb is to model those things that need to be standardized across the enterprise. First, this will be helpful because it will provide a single specification of the required functionality, and that specification can be reused by system implementation teams. This will save the implementation teams some work and will also minimize the chance that different implementation teams will create incompatible versions of the functionality. (If different implementation teams do create incompatible versions from the same enterprise model, that is a clue that the model may not be detailed enough.) Second, creating a single enterprise model of the functionality will make it easier to assess conformance across the enterprise because every implementation will be assessed against the same model.

For example, a common problem for users is that different systems require separate usernames and passwords; remembering all of them and which system each applies to can be challenging. To improve this situation, the corporation may decide that all systems will use a common authentication component. Creating a single model of this component at the enterprise level will save the individual implementation teams the work of creating such a model for use in their own designs.

The final rule of thumb I will discuss is deciding how big to make an individual model. This is a balancing act between having so many small models that managing them becomes difficult and having so few large models that each is too complex to be readily understood. In general, if something is a well-defined component and analyzing it by itself might be useful, then it is probably about the right size for a separate model.

Note that such a model need not be complex, provided it can answer the questions architects and managers need from the model.

When all is said and done, the most important thing to strive for when creating an architecture model is that it be useful. As George Box observed, your model will be wrong; that is just the nature of models. But just because a model is wrong does not mean that it is not useful. Making sure the model is useful is the architect's primary task.

All models are not created equal, and some models are more important to the enterprise than others. In addition, some models serve as foundational building blocks for creating other models. I divide enterprise architecture models into two main categories: primary objects and secondary objects. I describe each of these categories in the sections that follow, together with a high-level discussion of the models in that category.

# Primary Objects

Primary objects are those elements of the enterprise architecture that are absolutely essential. In effect, they are the "who, what, when, where, and why" of your architecture (the "how" will be determined by the emergent behaviors of the enterprise). If you do not have primary objects, it is difficult to say that you have an enterprise architecture in any meaningful sense. You may have a collection of models that describe parts of the enterprise, but you will not have an architecture that truly describes the enterprise.

I do not call these primary objects "models" because, strictly speaking, they may be expressed as elements of models rather than as stand-alone models in and of themselves. I will discuss the specifics of how these objects can be modeled in the following chapters; here my goal is to explain the reasons for creating these objects and their importance to creating an enterprise architecture that can be used as an effective operational management tool.

# Goals

Goals are the driving force behind an architecture, and yet most architecture frameworks neglect them. This neglect is the critical failure in the practice of enterprise architecture over the past few decades. If goals are not one of the primary objects of the enterprise architecture, it is likely that architects and managers alike will lose sight of them and be distracted by the details of the modeling process. The result of this distraction is often that the enterprise architecture effort becomes a niche activity that is irrelevant to the overall operation and management of the enterprise.

Stated plainly, goals are the "why" of the enterprise architecture effort. They define the reasons an enterprise architecture effort exists in the first place. There is no sense in undertaking an enterprise architecture effort merely for the sake of doing enterprise architecture. To ensure the entire effort does not degenerate into a jobs program for architects, it is vital that the enterprise architecture have clearly defined, measurable goals.[4] Any goal that is not measurable and that is not assessed on a regular basis is not achievable. It is human nature for people to pay attention to those things on which they are evaluated and to ignore things on which they are not.

There are two types of goals that an enterprise architecture needs to define: enterprise goals and architecture goals.

## Enterprise Goals

Enterprise goals are those goals that the enterprise wants to achieve. They are the reason that the enterprise architecture effort is undertaken in the first place. Why is the enterprise undertaking any given activity? To achieve some goal. The enterprise architecture is the place to define and document the enterprise's goals. These goals can be internally focused or they can be externally focused.

Internally focused goals are goals that describe some aspect of the enterprise's internal functioning that does not directly involve external organizations. With the effects of these goals felt through such things as increased efficiency, the results of achieving the goals may be invisible to any observer outside the enterprise. The goals may be business oriented; they may be personnel oriented; or they may be related to any aspect of the enterprise's functioning that is important to management.

An example of an internally focused goal would be a business wanting to save costs in its information systems budget by increasing software reuse and cooperation across system development teams. For example, instead of each implementation team independently purchasing a database product for its system's use, one goal could be that all systems will reuse a database product that was purchased at the corporate level for enterprise use. In addition to saving the cost of database licensing, the enterprise may also realize cost savings because a single database product requires a smaller staff as well as less specialized training.

---

[4]To create well-defined goals, use the SMART criteria defined in Chapter 2.

Externally focused goals are goals that describe some aspect of the enterprise's relationship to other organizations. The results of achieving these goals are directly visible to external organizations, and their effects will be apparent. These goals will generally be business oriented, though that may not always be the case.

An example of an externally focused goal would be increasing sales within a particular market segment. For example, a retailer may want to increase the proportion of its revenue that comes from online sales, or may want to increase its market share among younger customers.

The important distinction between internally focused and externally focused goals is that achieving externally focused goals is likely to require some interaction with organizations external to the enterprise, and that interaction may impose constraints on how the enterprise sets about achieving those goals. Internally focused goals generally give the enterprise more flexibility in how it goes about achieving them.

## Architecture Goals

Every activity that an enterprise undertakes should have some driving purpose. There is some reason the enterprise is devoting resources to that activity, and an enterprise architecture project is no different. But there is a problem in that while the architecture effort is focused on changing the enterprise, it is generally the case that the architecture effort never looks back at itself to see if it is having any measurable effect on the enterprise. It is entirely possible that an enterprise architecture effort could go on for years without having any effects outside the architecture team. The result is that an enterprise architecture effort often becomes a "self-licking ice cream cone"—a project where a lot of activity is visible, but the result is of no particular benefit to anyone.

To prevent this problem, it is important that the enterprise architecture project itself have some measurable goals. There must be some measurably useful result of the enterprise architecture effort. Most of the architecture goals will involve things that are of interest to the architecture team and management rather than the enterprise at large because management is the primary customer of the enterprise architecture team.

Put more formally, the enterprise architecture effort should be self-referential. The enterprise architecture should establish rules and constraints that it applies to the enterprise architecture effort itself, and its conformance to those rules and constraints should be measured and reported just as if the enterprise architecture effort were one of the system implementation efforts.

Examples of goals for the enterprise architecture effort include improving the interoperability among systems, increasing the consistency between architecture and design products produced by implementation teams (making it easier to review them), and understanding the effects each system in the enterprise has on achieving the enterprise's goals. The effects of the architecture goals will likely be visible only to the architecture team and management, although the implementation teams may notice some secondary effects such as spending less time justifying design decisions to the enterprise architecture team.

# Strategies

Having clear goals is a necessary precondition of any effort to improve, but a goal without a strategy for achievement is just a wish. If you want to realize any goal, you must have a strategy, in the form of a plan, that you will employ to increase your chances of achieving that goal.

For every goal that the enterprise architecture defines, there must be at least one corresponding strategy for achieving that goal. If a goal is the "why" of any activity the enterprise undertakes, then the strategy is the "what"—what actions the enterprise will take to achieve that goal. It is important to note that strategies are not detailed implementation plans; they are broad statements about large-scale actions. Once again, an analogy from military planning can be instructive.

Every military plan falls into one of three categories along a spectrum of detail: strategic, operational, or tactical. Strategic plans are those that express how an objective will be achieved over a relatively long term, often a number of years. Operational plans are smaller in scope than strategic plans, expressing how some subobjective within a strategic plan will be achieved. Operational plans usually have a scope measured in months or weeks. Finally, tactical plans are those day-to-day activities that address problems encountered while achieving an objective; they consist of the process that will be used to meet the operational and strategic goals. During World War II, the Allied *strategy* to defeat Nazi Germany was to invade Europe and defeat the Axis forces. One of the many concurrent *operational* plans was Operation Overlord, the amphibious landings at Normandy (other operational plans were part of the larger strategic plan, such as bombing campaigns and naval interdiction). Within Operation Overlord, a number of *tactical* plans were put into action: airborne troops were dropped behind Axis lines, infantry was landed on the beaches, ships bombarded Axis defensive positions, and so forth.

When formulating the strategy to achieve one or more enterprise goals, it is important to take a longer view of the situation. This is especially true if we are going to manage the enterprise architecture as a complex adaptive system. Any change made at the enterprise level will have effects on the emergent behaviors of the enterprise, but those effects will take time to manifest. Some effects may appear within a few weeks, but most will take months before they are visible.

It is important to keep in mind that effects caused by changes in the enterprise architecture cannot begin to emerge until enough time has passed for the changes to be reflected in the development and fielding of systems that were implemented after changes were made to the enterprise architecture.

# Actors

Having clearly defined goals and strategies for achieving them is important, but it is not sufficient to make progress toward achievement until each goal and strategy has one or more actors assigned to it. Actors may be individuals, organizations, or even systems. Anything that is capable of undertaking an activity is an actor, and actors may be internal to an enterprise or external.

Both goals and strategies are useless unless someone is responsible for implementing the strategies and achieving the goals. Those responsible must be represented in the enterprise architecture or it is not complete. More importantly, when assessing the enterprise's progress toward achieving its goals and the effects of the enterprise architecture, it is important that the progress be assessed in the right places. If one of the enterprise's goals is to increase sales in a particular segment of the market, it makes no sense to measure progress toward that goal by measuring how many system interfaces conform to international data standards. There is almost nothing a system implementation team can do to directly affect sales growth.

However, those responsible for achieving goals and implementing strategies do not act in isolation; there are many other actors on the stage and they must be considered as part of the enterprise architecture effort. System implementers may not be directly responsible for increasing sales (that is more likely to be a business development function), but if system implementers are taking actions that adversely affect sales growth, that is important to know. By the same token, identifying who is *not* involved in implementing a strategy or achieving a goal may be revealing. If the business development team is responsible for increasing sales in a given market segment, but no one from the advertising team is involved in the strategy for achieving that sales goal, that may be an indication that the strategy is flawed.

It is worth noting that actors are the units that make up the enterprise, the complex adaptive system that we intend to guide. While there are some individual actors who have specific effects on the enterprise (e.g., the chief executive officer), most actors function as part of the enterprise, and it is in the emergent behaviors of the enterprise that their actions are apparent. While each individual is an important and independent actor whose activities may affect the enterprise, our real focus is on the emergent behaviors of the enterprise as a whole.

## Processes

A good way to think of a process is as an idealized implementation of a strategy. A process is an expression of what we think a strategy will look like in practice. Processes define the sequence of activities that those who devised the strategy believe actors will need to implement to ensure the strategy is realized as envisioned and achieves the associated goals. While defining processes is important, keep in mind that many conceptions of processes do not survive first contact with the real world. As described in Chapter 2, emergent behaviors have a way of overcoming the intended processes regardless of how carefully they were devised. The point of this architecture framework is to help you recognize those situations and turn them to your advantage.

That said, all processes are not created equal. Some processes are really idealized strategies subject to change as emergent behaviors reveal themselves. But other processes, usually those related to some legal or regulatory requirement, are not idealized implementations but implementations that must be followed exactly to avoid placing the enterprise in legal jeopardy. When defining processes in your architecture, you should carefully denote which processes are required and the provenance of that requirement (such as the section of law that mandates the process).

It is tempting for senior managers to mandate some processes where there is really no reason for the current structure other than the fact that people are comfortable with the processes. These might be processes that have been handed down over the years with the justification "This is how we have always done it," or that were specified because a manager wanted to exert control over some aspect of the business. This temptation must be vigorously fought at every turn. The logic of "we have always done it this way" is deadly to any enterprise in today's dynamic environment.

The entire point of the enterprise architecture approach is that trying to define processes from the top down is counterproductive. To harness the inherent intelligence of any complex system, the actors must be free to innovate and find better ways to meet the enterprise's goals. Emergent behaviors cannot emerge in an environment that is controlled too tightly, and it is those emergent behaviors that we want to harness to our advantage. When new information becomes available, when environmental factors change, when new technology emerges, or when any other change to the status quo emerges, the enterprise must have the freedom to quickly respond to those changes.

# Data

It has been said that in the information economy, "Data is the new oil." Data is the lifeblood of any organization, whether it is a manufacturing firm, a government regulatory agency, or any other enterprise since time immemorial. As far back as ancient Mesopotamia, farmers could not profitably sell their crops if they did not know where to find potential customers. Weavers could not sell cloth if they did not understand what kinds of cloth people wanted to buy. Until recently, that data was captured primarily in written artifacts and in the minds of the organization's members. It was nearly impossible for any one person to access all of an organization's data, never mind synthesize it into an understandable whole. Small teams knew the data relevant to their portion of the organization and how it could best be leveraged to achieve their goals and complete their assigned tasks. Data analysis was a painstaking manual process undertaken by skilled specialists tasked with answering specific questions. Enterprise-scale data visibility and analysis was nearly impossible. But all that has changed over the past 30 years as large-scale storage and automated analysis have become commonplace, completely changing our relationship to data.

With the tools available today, storing vast amounts of data is a routine matter even for small businesses. And highly sophisticated data analysis that was previously the domain of skilled specialists is available through common off-the-shelf tools that can be effectively employed with only a few hours of training. Data analysis tasks that required custom tools and days of work only 20 years ago can today be accomplished in a few hours using commercial spreadsheet software. This new reality has unleashed a torrent of new data-driven business strategies, from microtargeted advertising to enterprise-scale efficiency initiatives.

These developments have led some to believe that it is possible to gain near perfect knowledge of the state of their enterprise since they have the tools needed to centrally manage and optimize all facets of their organization. The flaw in this thinking is that the same technology advances that have made it easy to store and analyze large quantities of data have also made it possible to accumulate ever increasing quantities of data. Our ability to gather and store data still far outstrips our ability to analyze and understand that amount of data. Data analysis largely remains a targeted task aimed at answering specific questions and revealing narrow slices of insight into the overall enterprise.

Improvements in our ability to analyze very large amounts of data are emerging, and maturing from research projects into commercially usable tools. In particular, advances in machine learning such as deep neural networks are making it possible to automate analysis tasks that could only be performed by a human as little as three or four years ago. However, machine learning is not some magical process that can just be thrown at large amounts of data and produce meaningful results. Data must be formatted and structured in a way that is suitable for the particular analysis technique being applied.

Regardless of the amount of data or the analysis technique, the data cannot be analyzed if the analysis tool doesn't understand both the syntax and semantics of the data. The syntax of the data may be apparent just by looking at it, but the semantics of the data may not be. Database table and column names may offer clues, but they are only clues and not reliable. Older databases may have had some fields repurposed— in a contact record, a field originally defined as storing e-mail addresses may have been repurposed to store Twitter handles, or the second line of an address field may include landmarks near the address. Even where data fields have not been repurposed, the clues provided by table and column names cannot be relied on in automated analysis. A computer must be told explicitly what the syntax and semantics of each data element is; it cannot adapt to unexpected input the way a human can. We need to model the data in a way that makes it possible for analysis tools to read and effectively use the data. Only by clearly and explicitly defining the syntax and semantics of the enterprise's stored data and the data exchanged among systems and external organizations can we unleash the power of automated analysis.

# Secondary Objects

The primary objects previously described are the absolute minimum needed to build an enterprise architecture. They are the fundamental building blocks that the rest of the enterprise architecture (and many system architectures) build upon. I call this next set of models "secondary objects" not because they are of secondary importance but because they cannot be adequately defined until the primary objects have been defined. This does not mean the primary objects need to be complete, but they do need to be specified with enough detail that they can be used to develop the secondary objects.

Like the primary objects, the secondary objects are not all full-fledged models. But those secondary objects that are not models themselves are integral parts of the models that will be created as the enterprise architecture matures and as it is reused by system development teams. With the primary objects as building blocks, creating the secondary objects begins to turn the building blocks into useful structures.

# Systems

While system implementation details should not be defined in an enterprise architecture, the existence of those systems and their relationships to other systems, goals, and elements of the enterprise architecture are vital to developing a usable enterprise architecture. If the purpose of an enterprise architecture is to understand and affect how an enterprise operates, then understanding the systems within the enterprise and their relationships is key to creating an enterprise architecture.

In an enterprise architecture, each system should be considered as an abstract thing, with no attempt made to capture its internal functioning, how it stores and manipulates data, or any of its implementation details. The important aspects of an individual system are its inputs and outputs, the effects it produces, and its relationship to rules and constraints. The system should be considered a discrete component that can be removed and replaced by any other system or capability that accepts the same inputs, generates the same outputs, and produces the same effects.

It is worth pointing out that I did not list conformance to rules and constraints as part of deciding whether one system can be replaced by another. Conformance to rules and constraints is not about whether one system *can* be replaced by another; it is about whether one system *should* be replaced by another. Whether one system should replace another is a judgment call that is part of the process of operating the enterprise. Conformance to the architecture's rules and constraints may vary over time as the system is updated (either through upgrade or a configuration change) or as the rules and constraints are updated. There may be reasons that the enterprise's management is willing to waive conformance for some systems; for instance, because the system is scheduled for a replacement with a system that will be conformant. Alternatively, the enterprise may be willing to change its rules and constraints to adapt to the realities of a given system implementation.

Because conformance to rules and constraints may vary over time, that information should be captured not by the architect manually modeling it but through the use of periodic assessments. Whenever possible, these assessments should be automated to ensure the results are repeatable and consistent as well as to improve efficiency. If the constraints are well formed, creating automated tests for each constraint will be relatively easy and will save the enterprise significant effort over the long run. I will discuss assessments in more detail in Chapter 7.

An important aspect of modeling a system at the enterprise level is to clearly and completely document its external interfaces. Any interface to the system that can be accessed by an external capability must be documented. One reason for this is that any available interface is a potential security vulnerability and understanding which security vulnerabilities exist is the first step in an effective security plan. More importantly, interfaces are the means by which systems are interconnected to implement processes. Interfaces are how other systems in the enterprise (and approved systems outside the enterprise) can access the data and functions provided by that system to help the enterprise achieve its goals; they are how the system receives its inputs and delivers its outputs. Any system with no external interfaces is by definition a stovepipe, and stovepipes are of limited usefulness to the enterprise.

The most important aspects in modeling a system within the enterprise architecture are capturing how that system contributes to the enterprise's goals and how that system fits into the enterprise's processes. If a system is not directly contributing to a goal of the enterprise or is not an important part of a process that contributes to a goal, then it is fair to ask why that system even exists.

# Behaviors

As discussed in Chapter 2, enterprise behaviors emerge from the interactions of all the elements of the enterprise, and the effects of these behaviors may be quite surprising. In practical terms, behaviors are the things that actors and systems actually do; they are the manifestation of processes and strategies. Where a process is an idealized implementation of a strategy, behaviors are the cold reality of how the enterprise is actually functioning and how that strategy is being carried out.

Because behaviors are things that spontaneously emerge in the enterprise, they cannot be modeled in the traditional sense of sitting down and specifying how the behavior will progress. Instead, behaviors must be captured from the actual functioning of the enterprise and its systems. Enterprise monitoring tools such as those used for cyberdefense can provide detailed information about how users make use of systems and how systems communicate with one another. System audit logs provide additional information about how systems are used and how data moves among systems within the enterprise and into and out of the enterprise.

Manually reviewing system logs and the output of cybermonitoring tools is difficult and time consuming, and it often requires specialized knowledge to understand the information. However, cybermonitoring tools and system logs usually generate carefully formatted data that can be captured and formatted as a workflow model. The resulting workflow models can be compared to the process models (provided they are captured in compatible formats) to gauge how well observed behaviors conform to the processes as originally conceived.

In some cases, particularly where conformance to a specified process is required by law or regulation, identifying these variations is an important part of the enterprise's ability to ensure compliance with those laws or regulations. In other cases, deviation from the original process may not be a cause for concern; it may be a cause for celebration. It is possible that a behavior is more efficient than the process as originally conceived. Alternatively, behaviors may reveal unexpected insights into how the enterprise functions. Behaviors may reveal that a system thought to be critical to achieving a particular goal may actually play no part in the enterprise's progress toward that goal, or they may reveal that more systems are involved in meeting a given goal than the architects originally believed.

As revealing as these captured behaviors may be, in most cases the behaviors themselves will not provide clear answers but instead provide clues about where the enterprise architects and managers should focus their attention to better understand what is actually happening in their enterprise and what factors are either contributing to the enterprise's ability to achieve its goals or inhibiting the enterprise from achieving those goals.

# Environment

At first glance, the idea of modeling the environment may sound intimidating. After all, the environment that an enterprise operates in is big, and that implies a large modeling effort just for that environment. But recall that modeling is all about abstraction—about creating a representation of something that is complete enough to answer the questions being posed, but not entirely faithful to the original.

Because the concept of an environment implies a very large, expansive set of things, it will help scope the discussion if we define *environment* before going any further. In discussing enterprise architecture, I don't use environment in the colloquial sense of "everything around us." I use it in the much narrower sense of "those things that have some effect on the enterprise but are outside the architect's control." This includes things like laws and regulations; other organizations the enterprise interacts with (including suppliers, customers, and competitors); and perhaps even economic forces and weather. For example, a bank's environment includes things like the federal, state, and local banking laws; the inflation rate; and interest rates set by the Federal Reserve, among other things.

In practice, your model of the environment will likely be rather small. Because modeling for the sake of modeling is a wasteful distraction, the environment model should only include those parts of the environment that have a direct effect on your enterprise. In a sense, you should treat the environment as just another system whose internal functions are hidden and all you know about it are the inputs you receive from it, the outputs you send to it, and the effects it produces. Keep in mind that company policies are also part of the environment, although in a healthy organization the enterprise architecture effort can drive changes in company policy, so to an extent company policy is not entirely outside the architect's control.

Modeling the environment is important because the environment has a number of direct effects on how your enterprise functions and whether it can achieve its goals using the planned strategies. The environment affects the enterprise's goals for the simple reason that many goals are defined with direct respect to the environment. For example, if one goal is to increase sales by some percentage, a number of environmental factors come into play. Can suppliers provide the raw materials needed to sell that many units? What effects will competitors' actions have? Are there regulatory concerns such as the need to satisfy consumer-safety regulations?

The environment affects processes and behaviors because the environment is where those things take place. The environment affects the behavior of the actors who carry out processes and exhibit behaviors. The environment will encourage some behaviors and constrain or prevent others. Environmental factors may make it impossible to carry out a process as first envisioned. This is equally true for those mandatory processes defined by law, regulation, or policy. Being able to document and quantify how the environment affects the enterprise's ability to carry out those processes may help efforts to change the process to make it more realistic. Ignoring the environment means ignoring one of the biggest influences on the enterprise.

Recall that effective modeling is largely a process of deciding where your model will be wrong. This is not always easy when modeling the environment because there are so many factors that may affect the enterprise. Some will be obvious, such as laws and regulations (which may be expressed as constraints). The effects of competitors' or suppliers' activities may not be as obvious or as easy to quantify, but they should at least be considered by the architecture team. It is likely that the list of environmental effects will vary over time as the enterprise changes and as the outside world changes. Like all aspects of enterprise architecture, this aspect will need to be reviewed and updated regularly.

# Standards

Standards are important in any enterprise because they improve interoperability by making it easier to integrate components produced by different teams. When two teams are building interfaces to the same standard, it is more likely they will be compatible (though it is not guaranteed). This is equally true of both hardware and software. Because the goal of a standard is to improve interoperability, it is at the interfaces of components that standards are most important to the enterprise architect. The interface and the information or product that flows across it are the standards that matter to an enterprise architect; standards employed inside the component are not the enterprise architect's concern. Knowing which standards are used in an enterprise and where they are applied helps the architect understand potential impacts of changing components or systems and also helps him or her identify situations where changes to the standard may have an impact on the enterprise.

Before going further, let me clarify what I mean by a standard. *Merriam-Webster* defines a standard as "something established by authority, custom, or general consent as a model or example."[5] In government and industry, *standard* usually has a more restrictive definition as a specification approved by a standards-setting body (of which there are many). Organizations such as the International Standards Organization (ISO), the Institute of Electrical and Electronics Engineers (IEEE), the Association for Computing Machinery (ACM), and many others publish a dizzying array of standards covering everything from the composition of alloys to the structure of computer languages. ISO alone publishes over 22,000 standards.

In theory, all of these standards help improve interoperability. And in many cases, they do improve interoperability. But as anyone who has built systems, particularly information technology systems, can tell you, just implementing a standard doesn't guarantee interoperability. Information technology standards often contain options or ambiguities that are implemented differently by different teams, effectively eliminating the benefits standardization is supposed to provide.

In practice, nobody really cares about the theory; they care about what gets the job done. And what gets the job done is whatever works in practice. Just because a given interface doesn't implement the ISO standard for the data being exchanged doesn't mean the interface must be changed. If the components communicating over that interface are performing well and are not adversely impacting other elements of the enterprise or the enterprise's ability to achieve its goals, there is no reason to change the interface to comply with the ISO standard. There may be very good business or operational reasons for adopting a commercial or international standard, but adopting a formal standard just to declare that your enterprise is "standards compliant" is the equivalent of modeling for modeling's sake.

In practical terms, a standard is whatever is working in your enterprise. Adopting a "corporate standard" or "organizational standard" doesn't imply any kind of inferiority with respect to adopting the specification produced by a standards-setting body, nor does it imply any superiority. What matters to the enterprise architect is that whatever shape the interface and the stuff flowing across it takes, it is well documented and available to other implementation teams. And that means it needs to be formally specified, with the precise syntax and semantics of each interface and the data or products that are consumed or produced by that interface.

---

[5]*Merriam-Webster*, 11th ed. s.v. "standard," https://www.merriam-webster.com/dictionary/standard.

As a general rule, an enterprise architecture effort will not need to create models of standards, because a well-defined standard has many of the qualities of a good model (the syntax and semantics will be well defined, often using a mathematically precise notation). Most times, linking the standard to the element that implements it will be sufficient. But every rule has its exceptions, and in some situations it may be necessary to create a model of a standard.

None of this should be interpreted as implying that adopting existing standards is a waste of time or effort. In many cases, adopting these standards will save a great deal of work and integration effort. Particularly with information systems, libraries that implement common standards are often readily available for reuse. My intent is only to emphasize that it is quite possible to be unduly focused on standards compliance, even to the point where architects lose sight of the original reason for adopting standards: to help the enterprise achieve its goals efficiently.

# Summary

The enterprise architecture framework described here adopts a fundamentally different approach to the task of building an enterprise. Instead of the traditional top-down approach that progressively decomposes high-level models to ever more concrete descriptions of the systems to be built, I describe a more limited approach that focuses on achieving the enterprise's goals.

The goal of enterprise architecture is to help the enterprise achieve its business goals, such as eliminating redundant systems or increasing market share. More concretely, the goal of enterprise architecture is to document the effects the enterprise wishes to bring about, the means by which the enterprise plans to achieve those effects, the resources required to achieve the effects, and the resources produced within the enterprise. This information should be explicitly captured in the enterprise architecture; indeed, that is the primary information that the enterprise architecture should contain. It is equally important to establish goals for the enterprise architecture effort itself so that the architecture team and managers can measure the effectiveness of the enterprise architecture effort.

The information in the enterprise architecture should be captured as formal models: mathematically precise descriptions that can be subjected to automated analysis. Diagrams may be useful for explaining concepts to senior managers and those without an engineering background, but they are too ambiguous to apply the automated analysis that is necessary to deal with the ever growing volume of data within an enterprise.

The purpose of modeling is to answer questions, questions that either the enterprise architect or the enterprise's management wish to have answers to. Models should be created to answer those specific questions, not for the sake of creating models. When creating those models, it is important to remember that all models, including the models that make up an enterprise architecture, are imperfect representations of reality. They do not need to capture all of the details of the thing being modeled; they only need to be detailed enough to answer the questions that were posed. Knowing what not to model is as important to an effective enterprise architecture effort as knowing what needs to be modeled.

When modeling, some models and model elements are more fundamental than others and form the building blocks that other models will reuse, whether they are part of the enterprise architecture or part of an implementation architecture. Establishing a good foundation early in the process will make it easier for others to create further models.

# CHAPTER 4

# Primary Objects

*When I was young, I had to learn the fundamentals of basketball. You can have all the physical ability in the world, but you still have to know the fundamentals.*

—Michael Jordan[1]

Primary objects are the main building blocks of any enterprise architecture. As I mentioned earlier, I call them "objects" instead of "models" because some of them are elements of models more than they are models in and of themselves. These objects are absolutely fundamental to constructing an effective enterprise architecture because it is only by defining each of these items in detail that your enterprise architecture effort has a chance of success.

In any field of endeavor, whether it is sports, business, music, or architecture, the people who are successful are those people who focus on the fundamentals of their craft.

Michael Jordan is one of the greatest basketball players to have ever stepped onto the court. His tremendous physical ability helped redefine the game in the late 20th century. What the epigraph highlights is what he considered the central pillar of his ability: absolute mastery of the fundamentals. He knew from hard experience that a person who has not mastered the fundamentals of their craft will not be able to develop more advanced skills. No amount of raw talent or innovative technique will make up for a failure to pay attention to the fundamentals.

The same rule that applies to individuals applies to organizations. If an automobile manufacturer cannot tighten nuts onto bolts, it will be unable to produce reliable cars, and no measure of innovative design will save the company from ruin. Enterprise architecture is no different; a solid mastery of the fundamentals of the task is the key to

---

[1]Michael Jordan, quoted in Ira Berkow, "Sports of The Times; Air Jordan and Just Plain Folks," *New York Times* "Sports," June 15, 1991, www.nytimes.com/1991/06/15/sports/sports-of-the-times-air-jordan-and-just-plain-folks.html.

© John D. McDowall 2019
J. D. McDowall, *Complex Enterprise Architecture*, https://doi.org/10.1007/978-1-4842-4306-0_4

success. And because the task of the enterprise architect is to help the enterprise achieve its objectives, the enterprise architect must master the fundamental elements of those objectives. Producing detailed models of systems, databases, and user interfaces is useless if the enterprise architect has lost sight of the original purpose of the enterprise architecture: to achieve the enterprise's goals. All else is merely a means to that end.

# Goals

As described earlier, goals should be the central focus of any enterprise architecture effort, both the goals of the enterprise as a whole and the goals of the enterprise architecture effort in particular. If meeting some definable enterprise goals is not the main focus of the enterprise architecture effort, then it is fair to ask why the enterprise architecture effort was undertaken in the first place. And if the enterprise architecture effort itself cannot articulate how it will be graded, then it will be difficult to judge if the enterprise architecture effort is effective. Goals are the means for deciding if the enterprise architecture effort is a success.

Business magazines are filled with cautionary tales of failed enterprise architecture initiatives and the need for dedicated support among key managers who are committed to change. Architecture conferences solemnly warn architects and managers that only by implementing the chosen framework thoroughly can they hope to avoid the same dismal fate. In reality, the problem is not about the framework, the dedication of the architects or managers, or resistance to change. It is not lack of dedication among the participants that dooms so many enterprise architecture initiatives. The problem is a failure to focus on the fundamental reason the enterprise architecture was started in the first place: to help the enterprise achieve its goals.

As an example, consider an enterprise architecture effort that employs the Zachman Framework. It starts at the "contextual" view of the enterprise and defines its goals as the "motivation" for the enterprise architecture. For as far as it goes, this is a good start. But as the architect works through the framework and develops the models for each cell in the framework, the amount of detail that the Zachman Framework develops becomes overwhelming for all but the smallest enterprises. The number of models that the architecture team has to develop and the level of detail that each model requires cannot be generated without significant effort. Furthermore, developing these models takes time. Given the pace of change in the modern enterprise, where Agile development and DevOps are the dominant system development paradigms, it is impossible for the architecture team to keep up. Rather than fight this losing battle, the architecture team is better off focusing on *whether* the enterprise is achieving its goals than on *how* the enterprise is achieving its goals.

The most critical step in achieving any goal is to define the goal in concrete terms that make it clear when the goal has been achieved or make it possible to measure progress toward achieving the goal. Amorphous goals like "Increase sales" are easy to utter, but they lack the specificity needed to readily measure concrete progress. The remainder of this section focuses on creating well-defined goals that can be applied within the enterprise architecture and used to measure improvements in the enterprise as a whole and the effectiveness of the enterprise architecture effort itself.

# Enterprise Goals

Enterprise goals are those goals that apply to the entire enterprise and are intended to improve its performance. Goals of this type are often called "business goals" even if the enterprise is not a corporation. The term *business* in this context just refers to the way the enterprise goes about its routine activities, and it applies equally to businesses, nonprofit foundations, government agencies, military organizations, or any other organized group of people and resources. The point of enterprise goals is that they apply to how the enterprise does its work and how it relates to the outside world.

The enterprise goals defined as part of the enterprise architecture effort must be goals that the effort can be reasonably expected to have some effect on. I think it is safe to say that most businesses have a goal of cutting costs. But it is difficult to see how any enterprise architecture effort, no matter how well implemented, can help cut the costs of office space used by staff. It is possible that a well-executed enterprise architecture effort will result in efficiencies or process improvements that lead to lower office space costs because it takes fewer people to do the same amount of work, but that is a second- or third-order effect. It can be very difficult to accurately attribute second- and third-order effects to their original causes because those causes are indirect. The goals documented for the enterprise should be those that can be directly measured, and their causes should be direct enough that strategies can be devised that will help achieve those goals.

Recalling the SMART[2] criteria discussed in Chapter 2, it is important that each goal be as specific as possible, and that each of its dimensions also be specific. For example, consider a goal of increasing sales. Sales can be measured either in terms of units sold or in terms of the dollar value of sales (assuming more than one product is being sold). Volume and dollar value are two different metrics that will be measured in different ways, and monitoring the enterprise's progress toward that goal will require gathering data. Counting the number of units sold isn't very helpful when your goal is to increase the dollar value of sales. Can you calculate the change in dollar value of sales from the number of units sold? Probably, but it would be easier and more accurate to just directly measure the dollar value and use that as your basis of performance assessment.

Goals must also be time-bound so that you know when to judge whether the enterprise has achieved those goals. While it is important that the goals themselves be realistic, it is also important that the time frames for achieving the goals are realistic. For example, while increasing the dollar value of sales by 25 percent in a single quarter might be an unrealistic goal, increasing the dollar value of sales by that amount over a year is within the scope of possibilities. Keep in mind that indirect effects generally take longer to manifest than direct effects. If you are implementing a new customer relationship management system in the first quarter of the year, it is unlikely that you will see any significant effect on sales in that quarter because it takes time to install and configure the software, to train users, and for users to learn how to work with the new system.

Because the intended use of goals is to measure the progress of the enterprise toward achieving them, goals should be expressed in a way that makes it easy to measure progress. In most cases, it should be possible to express the goal as an equation. Equations are easy for computers to understand and process, so expressing goals in this form makes it easy to automate assessment and reporting. Presenting goals as equations also makes it easier to incorporate the goals into enterprise architecture models, as equations are nothing more than a formal expression of some aspect of the model.

For example, if a corporation establishes the goal of increasing the dollar value of total sales by 20 percent in the next year, it could express that goal in this way:

$$totalSales_{currentYear} = totalSales_{previousYear} \times 1.20$$

---

[2]Specific, Measurable, Assignable, Realistic, and Time-bound

This equation provides a specific, measurable metric that can be used to gauge progress toward the goal. However, it is not enough to make this a complete goal. The goal must be assigned, meaning that the output of some system or process must produce the "totalSales" factor that will be evaluated. Whether or not the goal is realistic is a matter of judgment and depends on factors that must be evaluated by knowledgeable personnel on a case-by-case basis. The same applies to all of the SMART criteria except "Time-bound." While the current goal does specify that the measurement will consider total sales year by year, it does not specify how a year will be measured. This example should include a specific date range that the sales figures will cover, such as "All sales completed within one calendar year beginning January 1st." Depending on the nature of the enterprise, this seemingly simple goal may require a number of additional calculations and criteria. For example, a corporation with international sales may specify the currency units that will be used to measure sales, how exchange rates will be applied, or other clarifications that ensure everyone understands exactly what is being measured and how it is being assessed.

When formulating enterprise goals, keep in mind that goals are really an expression of what you expect the emergent behaviors of the enterprise to yield. The result consists of the effects the enterprise will produce based on the rules and constraints that have been defined, combined with the capabilities of the systems and the interaction of people with those systems. One simple way to think about which enterprise goals should be documented is to ask managers the question "What do you hope to get from all this investment of time and resources?"

# Architecture Goals

While the purpose of establishing and maintaining an enterprise architecture effort is to achieve the enterprise goals discussed in the previous section, just because the enterprise achieves one or more of its stated goals, it does not necessarily mean the architecture effort is the reason the enterprise achieved those goals. There is no way to judge the usefulness of the enterprise architecture effort solely on the basis of the enterprise achieving its goals because it is possible the enterprise might have been on the path to reaching those goals before the enterprise architecture effort was launched. The only way to determine if the enterprise architecture effort is worth the resources it consumes is to establish goals for the enterprise architecture effort itself, independent of the overall enterprise goals. For example, if one of the reasons senior leadership established an enterprise architecture effort was to increase commonality of components across systems, then one goal of the effort might be to reduce the number of relational database systems used within the enterprise. This is properly considered an enterprise architecture goal, and not an enterprise goal, because this goal is focused on how systems are built and fielded, not on what those systems do for the enterprise.

For many years now, an enterprise architecture effort has been seen as part of the cost of doing business, no different from paying for electricity or copy paper. It has been assumed that an enterprise architecture effort is necessary to help an organization improve its overall technical posture and efficiency, but the increasing skepticism of enterprise architecture among business leaders is proof that the benefits of enterprise architecture are not self-evident.

If the benefits of enterprise architecture are not self-evident, then we must have some way of determining whether the enterprise architecture effort is worth the resources it is consuming. To judge this, we need a means of measuring the architecture's achievements, and those means consist of established goals for the enterprise architecture effort to achieve.

There are a number of possible ways to measure the effectiveness of an enterprise architecture effort. The various models produced by the enterprise architecture team are probably the easiest measure to establish. And probably the most useless. As stated earlier, modeling for modeling's sake of is a waste of resources. And it is human nature that we will pay attention to those things we are being graded on. If the number of models is the means by which an enterprise architecture effort is measured, then the architects will ensure they get a good grade by producing large numbers of models. But the number of models tells you exactly nothing about the usefulness of those models or their contribution to the enterprise's ability to achieve enterprise goals.

Effective architecture goals must be derived from the enterprise goals previously discussed. If an architecture goal is not derived from an enterprise goal, there is no reason to believe that that architecture goal will contribute to achieving the enterprise goal in any meaningful way. By the same token, the enterprise architecture goals must be things the enterprise architecture effort can make a useful contribution to. For example, if one enterprise goal is to increase year-over-year sales, it would be inappropriate to establish an architecture goal of increasing engagement with potential customers in the 25- to 34-year-old age bracket. That is simply not a function of architecture. In contrast, an appropriate enterprise architecture goal that contributes to improving sales might be to document the process for creating, storing, and processing customer account information. This is relevant to enterprise architecture because understanding the way that information flows through the enterprise will help the marketing team ensure it is analyzing all available pertinent information when planning their advertising strategies. And documenting which systems capture, create, and store information, and the relationships among those systems, is certainly a function of architecture.

As is the case for enterprise goals, architecture goals should conform to the SMART criteria and must be measurable to be effective. But a key difference of the architecture goals is that they are not dependent on the emergent behaviors of the enterprise. Instead, the architecture goals are directly dependent on the actions of the enterprise architecture team. This means that progress toward these goals will be more obvious and can be measured more quickly than progress toward the enterprise goals. If the enterprise goals are strategic goals, the architecture goals are more akin to operational and tactical goals: they are focused on short-term objectives with limited scope.

When establishing architecture goals, it is best to avoid the trivial sorts of objectives that are easily met with little effort. Declaring that one architecture goal is that the enterprise architecture will be documented using SysML or a particular modeling tool is not an architecture goal, it is an implementation decision. Determining what kinds of models are necessary, naming patterns or other modeling conventions, and setting up version control procedures for the architecture are likewise implementation decisions.

Architecture goals should be focused on generating products or insights that are beyond those facts that can be ascertained through daily observation. One example of a useful architecture goal is documenting the profiles of exposed interfaces of all systems in the enterprise, as it provides two different but important pieces of information. First, it documents the potential integration points of all systems within the enterprise, making it possible to understand how systems can and do interact with one another and systems external to the enterprise. Second, this information provides a list of potential weaknesses in the enterprise's cyberdefenses, as any interface that is exposed to external systems presents an opportunity for an attacker to access the system.

Another example of a useful architecture goal is documenting the data flows across every system-to-system interface in the enterprise. This goal is closely related to modeling the data in the enterprise, as one of the purposes of this goal is to help understand the data flow through the systems in the enterprise.

One additional thing that should be considered is that it would be useful to understand the potential cost of not meeting the enterprise architecture's goals. That is, how much money is the enterprise wasting as a result of not controlling its enterprise architecture? Regardless of whether there is an enterprise architecture project, the enterprise has some architecture that is operating. It is likely an ad-hoc assemblage of systems and processes that has emerged organically over the course of years. But just because it emerged organically does not mean that it is either efficient or effective; an enterprise architecture project is an effort to make the enterprise architecture both more efficient and more effective.

Put another way, quantifying potential savings that an effective enterprise architecture effort would bring the enterprise is a useful goal, but a difficult one to capture accurately. Many factors will play into calculating this savings. Does the enterprise expect to save money by coordinating the purchase of software licenses in bulk? Does the enterprise expect to save operations and maintenance costs by updating legacy systems to more easily maintained baselines? These are difficult factors to quantify, but that does not mean they should be ignored. Indeed, saving costs is usually one of the main drivers of establishing an enterprise architecture effort in the first place, and if we cannot measure that costs savings, then it is difficult to justify the enterprise architecture effort.

There are any number of additional goals that could be established to gauge the effectiveness of the architecture effort. As with enterprise goals, these goals need to be measurable and time-bound; any assessment of the enterprise architecture effort's return on investment needs to be able to capture how well the architecture is meeting its goals, the cost of meeting those goals, and the ability to meet the goals on schedule.

# Strategies

Strategies are the means by which the enterprise plans to achieve its goals. They consist of the high-level activities the enterprise plans to undertake over a relatively long term, the resources that will be allocated to those activities, and the expected effects (i.e., the observable evidence of goals the strategy is supposed to achieve). Strategies are implemented over a relatively long term, usually at least one year. As a general rule, any set of activities whose effects will be visible in less than a year is more appropriately thought of as a process (described in the next section). Because of their broad scope and long-term focus, strategies usually involve multiple organizations within the enterprise.

Strategies are the initial step in making goals actionable. When you establish goals, you define some measurable achievement and assign some person or organization as the party responsible for achieving those goals. But that only defines what the enterprise intends to achieve; strategies define what the enterprise plans to do in order to achieve those goals as well. Strategies do not define the specific actions of individuals but rather the general actions of organizations, although in limited circumstances there may be a few individuals in key positions whose actions are critical to implementing a strategy. For example, suppose a relatively small manufacturer of jet engines has a goal of becoming a supplier to a large aircraft manufacturer. Part of the strategy for achieving that goal may be for the small company's CEO to recruit a business development manager who has an established relationship with senior managers at the aircraft manufacturer, making it easier for the engine manufacturer to develop a relationship with senior management of the aircraft manufacturer. This, in turn, will make it easier to present the engine manufacturer's capabilities and convince the aircraft manufacturer it is a viable supplier. While the CEO has specific actions to undertake as part of this strategy, it is unlikely the CEO can attract that business development manager unless the company as a whole presents itself well to the prospective hire. While the CEO's actions are important, they are not the whole strategy. Other elements of the strategy might include the human resources department putting together an attractive benefits package, the facilities manager making arrangements for upgraded office space for the new manager, and other actions that might factor into whether the prospective hire will accept an offer.

In most cases, strategies will not depend on the actions of a single individual or resource because strategies are inherently organizational functions. Any organization that regularly relies on specific individuals or single resources to achieve enterprise goals is engaged in behavior that puts the entire enterprise at risk. Relying on any one person or component introduces a single point of failure for the enterprise. Among software developers, when a project relies on a single individual for success, that situation is sometimes referred to as the project having a "bus factor" of one. This is a rather macabre metric that expresses the fact that if a single person (the critical individual) gets hit by a bus, the entire effort will fail because that person is so critical to the success of the effort that there is no one else on the team who can take over that person's duties. If your enterprise strategy has a bus factor of one, your strategy is deeply flawed.

A more robust approach is to develop strategies that rely on groups and organizations to complete the critical activities necessary to achieve the enterprise's goals. As a practical matter, this will likely entail establishing subgoals for each of those groups to ensure they are living up to the expectations of the enterprise and are meeting the expectations of senior management. However, keep in mind that for the moment we are discussing strategies, not processes. Subgoals and specific short-term activities are part of the processes that will be described in the next section. For now, we are focused on the strategy.

Strategies should be firmly grounded in reality—don't expect an enterprise architecture effort to have a direct effect on sales growth, for example. But a strategy that uses an enterprise architecture to improve information capture and sharing among the sales force can be expected to have that positive effect. When developing a strategy, it is important to be aware of what is feasible with the available resources and what is not. Adopting an unrealistic strategy is a sure way to set yourself up for failure.

Strategies do not lend themselves well to formal modeling because they do not have the level of detail normally required to create a well-defined formal model. But they do form the basis for creating processes; processes are the plan the enterprise will employ to execute the strategy.

# Processes

*Plans are worthless, but planning is everything.*

—Dwight D. Eisenhower[3]

Processes are the concrete steps that organizations, teams, and occasionally individuals take to support a strategy. Processes are an idealized description of the activities that architects believe must be completed to implement a strategy, who will complete those activities, and how those activities relate to one another both in terms of their ordering and in terms of the inputs and outputs of each activity. Every process is a plan for implementing all or part of a strategy, but plans rarely survive contact with reality. Once the enterprise implements a strategy, it will often find that the process cannot be carried

---

[3]Dwight D. Eisenhower, *Dwight D. Eisenhower 1957: Containing the Public Messages, Speeches, and Statements of the President, January 1 to December 31, 1957* (Washington, DC: US Government Printing Office, 1958), https://babel.hathitrust.org/cgi/pt?id=miua.4728417.1957.001;view=1up;seq=5.

out as originally envisioned. Unexpected external events, shortcuts or efficiencies that those doing the work discovered during execution, or any number of other factors may disrupt the process as originally conceived. That disruption is the sign of emergent behaviors in the complex system that is the enterprise.

If we intend to improve the practice of enterprise architecture by harnessing emergent behaviors, you may ask why you should bother defining processes. After all, if the emergent behaviors are how the enterprise actually functions, the process definition phase would seem to be a wasted effort. However, that overlooks the purpose of planning: to provide a means for senior managers to anticipate what resources will be required to implement a strategy, who will need those resources, and when those resources will be needed. Undertaking any complex activity without an initial planning step is setting yourself up for failure.

US Army General Dwight David Eisenhower was the supreme allied commander in Europe during the Second World War. In this position, he was responsible for the implementation of the Allied strategy for defeating Hitler, and he had overall responsibility for the planning and execution of the D-Day landings at Normandy on June 6, 1944. When he said that "plans are worthless, but planning is everything," the point Eisenhower was trying to make is that no plan will be executed as first envisioned because reality and events will intervene, and the initial plan will be modified to deal with those circumstances as they arise; in retrospect, the actions that were taken may not resemble the original plan at all. But, as Eisenhower considered it, it is in the act of planning that the leader thinks through the hoped-for course of action and analyzes the resources that will be needed at each step along the way. The leader also thinks through contingencies—the ways the plan could go wrong or events could disrupt the plan. By thinking through these contingencies, the leader can develop options for dealing with those circumstances as they arise and build them into the original plan. It is much easier to deal with a problem you anticipated and planned for than to deal with a problem that you did not consider. This is why it is important for architects and senior managers to plan out processes that will be used to implement strategies.

## Process Example

Processes defined in the enterprise architecture do not need to be specified in an excruciating level of detail, especially since it is a given that the process will not likely be executed as originally designed. But they do need to be specified with sufficient detail to define the major activities that will be performed as part of the process, any necessary ordering among those activities (e.g., activity A precedes activity B), the party that is responsible for performing each activity, and the expected inputs and outputs of each activity. An example process model is depicted in Figure 4-1.

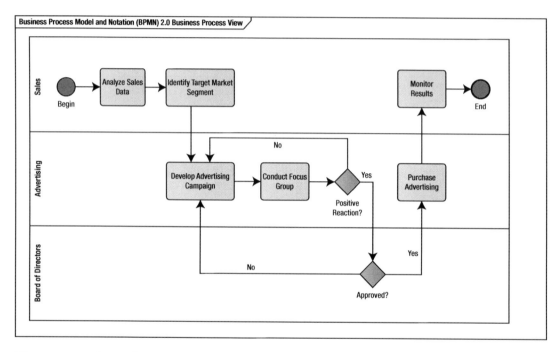

***Figure 4-1.***  *Sample Process Diagram*

The model in the figure depicts a simple process for developing an advertising campaign that targets a new market segment. The model is expressed using the Business Process Model and Notation (BPMN) 2.0 language.[4] BPMN is a process-modeling language developed and maintained by the Object Management Group, an industry consortium that promotes the use of formal modeling languages and the adoption of model-based engineering. While BPMN is primarily a graphical language, it has a formal underlying syntax and semantics that make it possible to apply automated analysis techniques to BPMN models.

---

[4]"About the Business Process Model and Notation Specification Version 2.0," Object Management Group, www.omg.org/spec/BPMN/2.0/, January 2011.

In BPMN, a solid circle is used to denote the start of a process. Put another way, the symbol (i.e., syntax) of a solid circle carries the meaning (i.e., semantics) of denoting the beginning of a process. Each symbol in the language has a similar formal syntax and semantics. For example, a diamond shape, called a "gateway," represents a decision point and only a decision point; it cannot be used to represent any other type of activity. BPMN supports much more complicated syntax and semantics than are depicted in this model. There are several types of gateway symbols representing an "exclusive or" decision (i.e., only one path may be chosen), a split into parallel execution paths, and other decisions that are useful in developing sophisticated business process models.

The diagram shown in Figure 4-1 is divided into three rows called "swim lanes." Each swim lane represents a different actor in the process; any symbol within a participant's swim lane is the responsibility of that actor. Arrows between activities represent the flow of the process (more complex diagrams may include arrows that represent the flow of data or other nuances of the process).

In this simple process, we can see that the sales department will analyze sales data and then identify a new market segment it wants to target for increased sales, improved brand awareness, or some other reason. The advertising department will develop a new marketing campaign designed to address the sales department's needs and will test the new campaign with focus groups. If the focus groups have a negative response, the advertising team will go back and redevelop the marketing campaign. This cycle may repeat several times until the focus groups have a positive response to the marketing campaign. After receiving a positive response from the focus groups, the board of directors will decide whether or not to proceed with the campaign. It may send it back to advertising for redevelopment or may approve the campaign. Upon approval, the advertising team purchases advertising and the sales team monitors results. This ends the process.

The process just described is only a simple process to illustrate a concept. But a process model within an enterprise architecture should not be significantly more complex. Remember, the point of the process model is for the architecture team and senior managers to think through the plan for executing some strategy. They will need to consider which organizations within the enterprise need to be involved, who the critical decision makers are, what the major activities are, and the anticipated flow of events. Once this plan has been thoroughly considered and documented, the enterprise has the information necessary to begin managing its execution of the strategy for increasing its market share. It has the tools to observe the behaviors of the enterprise and compare those behaviors to the process as originally envisioned, but more importantly to the results the enterprise achieves.

The process model forms the initial baseline for governing the enterprise. For example, the advertising team may find that it is more effective to engage with focus groups before developing any marketing campaign materials. Alternatively, while monitoring the results of the new advertising campaign, the human resources department may realize that something about the advertising campaign is making the company a more attractive employer for engineers. These results were not anticipated by those who designed the process, but they are important emergent behaviors that should be recognized by the enterprise architecture team and senior management. This is exactly the sort of emergent behavior we want to leverage. Only by observing the actual results can we capitalize on that information to improve process models and make better use of the enterprise's resources. For example, future advertising campaigns may include focus groups of engineers to gauge whether the campaign will have a positive or negative effect on recruiting.

The emergent behaviors I have discussed here are generally positive, but keep in mind that negative emergent behaviors may also emerge. For example, the enterprise may notice that when a new advertising campaign is in development the sales team reduces its engagement with potential customers, holding off on aggressively pursuing leads until the new advertising materials are ready. These negative emergent behaviors are at least as important as the positive emergent behaviors and should likewise be monitored and used for continuous improvement.

# Required Processes

As a general rule, processes should initially be modeled without too much detail and with the expectation that the process will organically change as new behaviors emerge in the enterprise. However, all processes are not created equal. While most processes defined in the architecture are guidelines and planning relics, there may be some processes whose execution must follow the defined process exactly to avoid adverse legal or business consequences. For example, government agencies have strict records-management policies that govern how the information they produce must be handled, protected, and preserved. These records-management policies are encoded in law and regulation and must be strictly followed; some of them are very specific in how certain types of documents must be handled to protect the privacy of individuals whose information is in the documents.

There may be other instances where specific processes must be followed exactly to conform with corporate policy that is tied to some external requirement. For example, software development projects that implement the Capability Maturity Model Integration (CMMI) process improvement program may have specific procedures to follow in order to conform to the higher-level CMMI assessment criteria. Failure to follow the documented procedures can jeopardize the organization's CMMI assessment.

In cases where processes must be followed as written, that information should be noted as part of the process model. It is advisable to note the instruction prominently to ensure that provenance is clearly understood. Any assertion that a set process must be followed due to law, regulation, organizational policy, or some other reason should include a specific provenance for that assertion, such as the paragraph in the relevant policy document. This provenance information is important because people are more likely to appreciate the importance of following the process if the reason is clearly spelled out. "Because management said to do it this way" is not a compelling reason for people to follow specific processes.

Provenance information is also important in allowing those implementing the process to know how to go about changing parts of the process that may be outdated or inefficient where possible. Among the emergent behaviors in the enterprise may be instances where processes that are required by government regulation can be done more efficiently, and it may be possible to work with regulators to define a better process that still meets the regulators' needs. Or perhaps there is a more streamlined way to implement some process defined by organizational policy; it is helpful if those doing the work know which policy needs to be updated so they can discuss that option with the group that produced that policy.

Regardless of the actual provenance of any process, it is important to review the processes from time to time. Having some defined schedule for architects and managers to review processes (e.g., annually) ensures that all processes get reviewed regularly and remain up to date. In addition, some critical processes might be designated for specific event-based reviews. For example, new tax legislation might drive a review of all processes related to financial reporting. In addition, security policies change frequently due to the rapidly evolving nature of the cyberthreat, and no enterprise can afford to have out-of-date security processes driving the organization.

# Actors

Actors are the individuals or groups that execute processes, implement strategies, and either do or do not achieve the enterprise's goals. They are the agents whose interactions result in the emergent behaviors we seek to take advantage of to modernize the practice of enterprise architecture. Importantly, actors may be living, sentient creatures (i.e., humans or groups of humans) or they may be nonhuman things. Information systems, animals, even the weather—anything that can have some independent effect on the enterprise—may be considered an actor. And because actors are the entities whose interactions determine whether the enterprise achieves its goals, it is important to model actors as part of our enterprise architecture.

In the world, actors exist at many levels of abstraction. At the lowest level, actors are all individuals, whether individual living beings or systems. Individuals either do or do not complete specific activities, and those activities affect whether the enterprise achieves its goals. But higher-level aggregations of those individuals are also actors; the collective action of the aggregations also has an effect on whether the enterprise achieves its goals regardless of how each individual in that organization acts. For example, an aircraft manufacturer purchasing engines from a supplier has an interest in whether the supplier provides the proper engine on the agreed date. The activities of any given individual working for the supplier are irrelevant from the aircraft manufacturer's point of view; all the aircraft manufacturer cares about is whether the engine supplier as an organization delivers engines on time and within budget.

In most cases, an enterprise architect will be more concerned with the activities of groups and roles than the activities of specific individuals. This is not universally the case; as discussed in the "Strategies" section, there may be some key individuals whose actions have such an influence on organizational performance that they should be modeled as individuals.

If the architect is going to model actors as groups, deciding what size group to model becomes a key consideration. There are no hard-and-fast rules that can be readily applied to this decision, but a good practice is to model actors at the lowest level of granularity where their actions as a group have a significant effect on the execution of the process or strategy. For example, consider the case of a software development project that has been underway for a number of years. The systems and teams that develop and deliver the product are already in place and performing, but you want to model their process for creating a security patch for the product. The process could be modeled as one actor, the "product development team." But this will tell you little about how the process is actually implemented. It would be more appropriate to model the actors at a lower level of granularity, perhaps by distinguishing them as the system engineering team, the software development team, and the testing team. Each of these groups has distinct activities that they perform when developing a security patch for the system, and their responsibilities are different enough that understanding how each team performs is of interest when analyzing organizational behavior. But modeling the planned activities of each individual software developer or tester would be needlessly complex and time consuming.

If you must model individuals, model them as roles and not as named individuals (e.g., "Corporate Compliance Officer" rather than "Susan Smith"). Primarily, this reduces the likelihood that the model will need to be updated due to personnel turnover or reassignment. But it is also important because as the behaviors emerge from the enterprise, we may see a shifting of actions among the different people, or two roles that were performed by one person getting split across two people, or several people being authorized to perform the duties of a given role. In these cases, while the action is performed by a single person, it is that person's role within the organization and the process that is of interest to the architect.

# Data

Data modeling has long been almost exclusively the concern of database architects and software developers. It has been viewed as something necessary for those doing the implementation work but as less important for those trying to direct that overall operations of the enterprise. This view may have been acceptable years ago, when large, monolithic systems were designed to operate independently and data analysis was something that systems did on their own data. In recent years, this has all changed with the increase in processing power and the improvement in large-scale data analysis techniques that have made enterprise-scale data analytics not only a reality but a necessity.

It has been said that "data is the new oil." I agree with this analogy and apply it in two ways. First, oil is a lubricant that helps mechanical systems operate more efficiently by reducing the friction between moving parts. In an analogous way, making data more readily available within and across organizations can smooth the functioning of those organizations because people can more easily access the data they need to complete their assigned tasks more accurately and efficiently. Second, oil is a commodity of immense value because it is critical to many industries. By the same token, in today's information economy, data is a commodity that is critical to many organizations.

John D. Rockefeller established the Standard Oil Company in 1870, which rapidly established control of most of the US oil market; in 1911 the US Supreme Court ruled that the company was an illegal monopoly and ordered it broken up. During this period, the internal combustion engine was rapidly being developed and the industrial economy was making the transition from animal power to engine power. This transition required ever increasing amounts of petroleum products to continue growing. Rockefeller made a fortune by controlling the supply of oil. In the same way the industrial economy of the early 20th century needed ever increasing amounts of oil, our information economy consumes ever increasing amounts of data. We have a rapidly increasing ability to analyze ever larger volumes of data and apply the results to market analysis, process improvement, and many other pursuits.

Entirely new industries have risen up around our ability to gather and rapidly analyze large volumes of data. Companies such as Google, Facebook, and Twitter base their entire business model on the ability to gather large amounts of data, analyze it quickly, and apply the results. The proliferation of electronic devices from smartphones to security cameras has resulted in an exponential increase in the amount of data any enterprise gathers and has access to. Those who cannot analyze the data in their enterprise will find themselves at a severe competitive disadvantage and those who can make use of that vast ocean of data will be able to adapt and respond quickly to changing circumstances and business needs.

The increasingly large amounts of data that are available for analysis have grown to the point we cannot do the analysis manually. Cameras regularly generate more than a terabyte of video each day, and geolocation sensors on vehicles can generate thousands of location reports in a matter of hours. To be effective, we must automate as much of the analysis as possible. Automating data analysis means that we must document the data in a format that our analysis tools can understand.

There are two states of data that are of interest to the enterprise architect: the data that is stored by the enterprise (data at rest) and the data that is exchanged between different systems across interfaces (data in motion). Regardless of which state of data you are modeling, all data should be modeled the same way.

# Syntax and Semantics

In order to analyze any piece of data, we need to understand both the syntax and the semantics of that data. If you know the format of data but not its meaning, then any analysis will be, quite literally, meaningless. If you know the meaning of a piece of data but not its format, you will find it difficult or impossible to analyze the piece of data. As a simple example, consider a piece of data that represents the latitude of a geospatial position. Latitude can be represented in any of several ways. Consider the following example, where each item depicts the same measurement of 42° north latitude:

- *Degrees minutes seconds*: 42° 20′15″

- *Degrees decimal minutes*: 42° 20.25′

- *Degrees decimal*: 42.3375°

There are also many other possible representations. This example assumes that positive numbers represent north latitude and negative numbers represent south latitude. This is a common convention, but unless that convention is explicitly stated, the specification is ambiguous. Assuming an analyst "just knows" what that the data follows some convention can lead to incorrect analysis if the assumption is faulty. Different user communities may use different conventions. It is possible that the encoding system uses $N$ to denote north latitude and $S$ to denote south latitude. That would mean these values are incomplete and cannot be correctly interpreted. There are many additional possible means of encoding latitude coordinates: Universal Transverse Mercator, Military Grid Reference System, and others. Each of them is accurate; each of them is translatable to the others; and each of them can be used in analysis. They all have the same semantics, but vastly different syntax. By the same token, the string "New York" may refer to the state in the northeastern United States; the city in the northeast United States; or a community in Lincolnshire, United Kingdom, or any of several other municipalities in the world. In this case, the syntax is identical but the semantics vary significantly.

## Modeling Data

When we think of data, we may think of a number of different formats: word-processing documents, spreadsheets, Extensible Markup Language (XML) documents, databases, log files, video, still images, audio recordings, and many other means of storing information. While it may seem like there are a dizzying array of means for storing data, we can divide data into some basic types that facilitate modeling.

Most discussions of data refer to it as "structured," "semistructured," or "unstructured," but these terms are both inexact and somewhat misleading. The term *structured data* is generally used to refer to relational databases, where data is formatted as rows and tables with formal relationships and a standardized means of being queried such as the

Structured Query Language (SQL). The term *semistructured data* is usually used to refer to XML files or other file types where the structure of the data may be formally defined (e.g., by using an XML schema definition) but the data is not as rigidly structured as it is in a database. This kind of data can often be queried with a language such as XQuery or readily parsed into useful elements using such techniques as regular expressions. And the term *unstructured data* refers to word-processing documents, presentations, and similar formats that cannot be readily queried or parsed using standard techniques but generally require a human reader to interpret them.

These traditional divisions of data have a number of flaws. To begin with, the definition of semistructured data is notoriously inexact, and may encompass multiple formats. (In fact, some authorities do not consider "semistructured" to be a valid description at all.) Furthermore, it can be persuasively argued that much of what is referred to as unstructured data actually has a very definite structure. Many documents that are produced on a periodic basis follow the same format every time. For example, military operations orders are created as word-processing documents, but they have a specific structure that they follow. If we are to formally model data in a consistent way that lends itself to automating data analysis, we must have a more concrete means of describing data.

If we step back and examine data in all its varied forms, we can identify two fundamental ways data is structured: as tuples or as objects. A tuple is just an ordered set; tuple is the formal term used by mathematicians and data engineers to describe data that is essentially stored as rows within tables. Every database and spreadsheet is composed of tuples, as are most XML documents, log files, and other data that is captured as a series of discrete elements that can be individually retrieved using SQL or similar tools. Where discrete elements are not readily retrievable, the data is best considered as an object—a pile of information that requires sophisticated machine-learning techniques or human interpretation to understand the data and retrieve useful pieces of information from it.

## Tuple Data

Tuple data lends itself very well to formal modeling. A number of techniques are available to the data modeler. The most common may be Data Definition Language (DDL), the language used to define the structure of a relational database. DDL is a good modeling language for relational databases, but its ability to express semantics is severely limited. Similarly, the XML Schema Definition Language (XSD) is a good language for defining XML documents, but in addition to having severe limitations with regard to modeling semantics, it is only suitable for modeling data encoded as XML.

When modeling tuple data, I find that the Web Ontology Language (OWL) is an excellent language for modeling tuple data. For one thing, OWL was specifically designed to capture both the syntax and the semantics of data. Furthermore, OWL is derived from Description Logics, a family of formal knowledge representation languages. This makes it possible to use automated tools to reason over the data and even infer new facts from the available data. More importantly, because OWL can formally describe both the syntax and the semantics of tuple data, when OWL is used to describe data, we can create models that have all the necessary detail to enable automated analysis of the data.

## Object Data

Object data is more difficult to model with the same level of detail as tuple data. The main reason is that the semantics of individual pieces of data (paragraphs, graphics, etc.) are very complex and may depend greatly on the context—the proximity of other sentences, phrases, or other portions of the data. I used the term "object" because there are data types available in many relational databases called Character Large Object (CLOB) or Binary Large Object (BLOB). CLOB data refers to objects that are stored as an undifferentiated collection of printable characters; BLOB data refers to objects that are stored as binary files such as images.

The best way to model object data is with the file format definitions used to store the data (in the case of data at rest) or to stream the data (in the case of data in motion). The vast majority of object data is captured in a file that follows some published standard. Images may be stored using the Joint Photographic Experts Group (JPEG) format, the Portable Network Graphics (PNG) format, or many other imagery formats. These formats are well defined, and most have a number of commercial or open-source libraries that can be used to read, write, and process them. The same is true of most formats that are used to stream data across a network. Keep in mind that the only real difference between streaming data and file data is that a file is just a stream that has been saved to disk.

These data file formats define the syntax of the data very well, but they are not intended to capture the semantics of the data because the data's semantics are completely independent of its syntax. For example, a JPEG image may be a picture of a car, a picture of a human, or a picture of a map. Nothing in the format of the data file can tell us anything about the semantics of that data (although in some cases amplifying character data can be embedded in the file to provide some descriptive information).

A document may be an intelligence report, a news summary, or the results of a horse race; nothing about the format of the file tells us anything about the meaning of the contents.

Many publications discuss how to store *metadata*—that is, data about data, usually referring to some kind of tuple data that captures information related to an object. For example, a word-processing document may have associated metadata that captures the title, author, subject, publication date, and other relevant information about the file. I do not believe that metadata actually exists; it sets up a false dichotomy. One person's data is another person's metadata; it should all be treated as something that can be usefully analyzed. In reality, metadata is just a role that one piece of data takes in relation to another piece of data. If the item of interest is a report, the name of the author is metadata about the report. If the item of interest is a person, a document authored by that person is metadata about that person. What is important, regardless of what you call it, is that you model the information in a way that captures both its syntax and semantics in a format that can be used to help automate the analysis of that data.

## Summary

Primary objects are the fundamental building blocks of an enterprise architecture. Most of them are not architecture models as such but are key building blocks that will be used in creating detailed architecture models. Without a solid foundation of fundamental structures to build on, the enterprise architecture effort will have a difficult time developing the models necessary to monitor the enterprise and assess the enterprise's progress toward its goals.

Goals should be the starting point for any enterprise architecture effort. If the enterprise cannot describe the things it wants to accomplish, then no amount of modeling, monitoring, or any other activity will help the enterprise improve. The most obvious type of goal is the enterprise goal: something the enterprise wishes to accomplish. Improving the chances of reaching an enterprise goal should be the main reason for establishing an enterprise architecture effort in the first place. In addition to enterprise goals, it is important to establish specific goals for the enterprise architecture effort itself. These goals should be derived from the enterprise goals and support the enterprise goals, but they should be goals that the enterprise architecture effort itself seeks to achieve. If we do not measure the achievements of the enterprise architecture effort in and of itself, then we have no way of judging whether the enterprise architecture effort is contributing to the enterprise's progress toward its goals or if it is having no effect (or perhaps even having a negative effect).

Strategies are the high-level means by which the enterprise intends to achieve its goals. They are relatively long-term activities, typically taking a year or more to come to fruition. They are not highly detailed and usually describe the activities of groups rather than individuals. Strategies are, in effect, the means for organizing processes into manageable groups. Their high-level nature makes it difficult to create models of them that are useful enough to justify the cost of their creation and maintenance.

Processes are the more detailed short-range plans executed by the enterprise. They are readily modeled using techniques such as BPMN. Processes are idealized expressions of how the enterprise plans to achieve one or more goals. As a general rule, these models should not be too detailed because we do not expect them to survive contact with reality. The emergent behaviors of the enterprise will reveal new means of achieving the enterprise's goals. Sometimes they do this by conveying more efficient means of achieving the goals than were envisioned by the enterprise architecture team that created the process models, and sometimes they do it by showing effects that were not anticipated or participants that were not an obvious part of the process at the time the process model was created.

Actors may be individual persons, systems, or groups of people. It is actors that perform the activities that make up process models, and it is the interactions of actors with one another and with their environment that result in the emergent behaviors that we seek to take advantage of in managing an enterprise architecture. Actors should be modeled as roles and not as named individuals. This makes it easier to maintain models over time despite personnel turnover or shifting responsibilities across the enterprise.

Data is one of the most valuable resources of any enterprise and understanding the enterprise's data should be one of the primary tasks of the enterprise architecture effort. Data may be at rest (stored) or in motion (exchanged among systems). Regardless of whether data is at rest or in motion, it is important to model both its syntax and semantics in a formal manner that makes it possible to use automated tools to process and analyze the data with minimal human intervention.

# CHAPTER 5

# Secondary Objects

I call the objects described in this chapter "secondary" because it would be difficult to create any of them without first creating the primary objects. They are not secondary in importance; as explained in later chapters, they are, to a very large extent, the real heart of the enterprise architecture. But they are secondary in terms of when and how they are created. The secondary objects build on the primary objects and extend them from simple building blocks into proper architecture models that can be used to manage the enterprise and guide it toward achieving its goals.

The objects described in this chapter can all be captured as real models. Where some of the primary objects are little more than guideposts and framing constructs, the secondary objects are true models, with all the complexity and precision necessary to make them useful subjects of analysis. Where the primary objects are the fundamentals, the secondary objects are applications of those fundamentals.

There are many options available for creating the models described in this chapter. All of them could be captured in SysML, which is a good all-around system modeling language. Modeling them in UML is another possibility, although the UML lacks some of the expressiveness that is helpful in defining these models. In reality, nearly any formal modeling language, including OWL, Common Logic, and many others, can be used to model these objects. As this is not a book about modeling, a detailed discussion of the modeling options and trade-offs is not appropriate here. It is enough to state that the specific modeling language or tool is unimportant as long as these objects are created as proper models, using a formal modeling language that is expressive enough to do the job right and enable automated analysis.

When creating these models, it is important to keep in mind that the purpose for doing so is to help guide the enterprise toward achieving its goals. Any model that does not contribute to that metagoal is a distraction.

© John D. McDowall 2019
J. D. McDowall, *Complex Enterprise Architecture*, https://doi.org/10.1007/978-1-4842-4306-0_5

# Behaviors

Behaviors are one of the enterprise architect's main interests. In particular, it is the emergent behaviors of the enterprise as a complex system that are of interest. Behavior models are a representation of how the enterprise is actually functioning regardless of what management wants, what the architecture team expected, or any other preconceived notion. Behavior models need to represent real-world activities and events to the maximum extent practicable; that is, they need to represent how the enterprise is behaving with enough fidelity to understand how the actors' interactions with one another, with systems, and with the environment are producing the observed effects.

Because it is the observed effects that we are most interested in, effects are the main focus of creating behavior models. It is not necessary to capture every detail of each activity the participants take part in, as most of those details will be irrelevant to the ultimate effects. But some of those details may be critical to producing the observed effects, and it is difficult to know which details will be critical before you create and analyze accurate behavior models. This is one of the main reasons that creating behavior models is an iterative process that is never truly complete. Just because you have captured an enterprise behavior in a model does not mean you have enough fidelity to understand the critical factors that are driving that behavior. In practice, you really won't know if you've captured the critical factors until you implement some new rule or system feature to try to change the behavior and observe whether the behavior changes (or does not change) as a result of that rule or feature.

Another reason that capturing behaviors is an iterative process is because enterprises are dynamic entities whose behaviors change over time. Just because you have captured an enterprise behavior in March does not mean you still have an accurate representation of that behavior by November. New people and systems will be added to the enterprise, people's roles will change, and other drivers will have an impact on the emergent behaviors of the enterprise. Old behaviors and their resulting effects may disappear entirely, or be replaced by completely new behaviors and effects. Other behaviors may continue to go along as before, seemingly impervious to changes of personnel or systems, and their effects likewise continue unchanged. As discussed earlier, one of the critical characteristics of emergent behaviors is that they are not readily predictable, so these changes will often be unanticipated.

A good example of this comes from my time flying helicopters for the Marine Corps. Into the early 1990s, when there was a problem with an aircraft, the crew filled out a paper Maintenance Action Form (MAF), a form with four color-coded carbon copies plus the original. The colors were designated for specific purposes: one color would go to the work center that performed the maintenance, another color would go to the quality assurance division, and so forth. This color-coding system allowed the maintenance control division to track the status of any aircraft's maintenance activities by glancing at the colors showing on its status board. In the mid-1990s, the Marine Corps fielded a computerized maintenance system where crews would type the information on the MAF into a computer and the system would automatically route the information to the appropriate work center, eliminating the need to track five pieces of colored paper. What nobody anticipated was how the maintenance controllers would respond. The computer system only displayed text; it had no color coding and so it took longer to understand each aircraft's status. So, the maintenance controllers printed five paper copies of each MAF, marked them up with highlighters of five different colors, and continued on as before.

Capturing the behaviors of the enterprise sounds like an enormous task requiring a great deal of effort. At first glance, this may seem like an intimidating amount of work for uncertain benefits. But recall that the entire enterprise architecture effort should be devoted to helping the enterprise achieve the goals documented earlier. We are not trying to capture all the behaviors of the enterprise; we only want to capture those behaviors that have a direct effect on those goals that we documented. For example, if one of the enterprise goals is to increase sales of current products by 20 percent, then capturing how the sales team interacts with and records information about prospective customers is important, but capturing how the sales team works with the new product development team is not. There are many other behaviors that may emerge in the enterprise, but those are of little interest to the enterprise architect. They may be of interest to system architects, but that is a different matter that is best handled as part of the system architecture efforts for each of those systems. The individual system architecture teams may be able to reuse the information captured by the enterprise architecture effort, but that is not the primary concern of the enterprise architecture team.

The most straightforward way to decide which behaviors to document is to work backward from the enterprise goals. Pick a goal, identify the observable effects that indicate whether the enterprise is making progress toward achieving that goal, and begin documenting the behaviors that produce the observable effect. If the desired effect is not observed in the enterprise (i.e., it appears the enterprise is not progressing toward that goal), then there must be some observable effect that indicates the enterprise is not achieving that goal—an undesirable effect. Use this effect as the starting point for modeling the behavior that creates it; from there, you can begin working on changing that behavior to produce a more desirable effect.

# Capturing Behaviors

If we want to accurately capture the behaviors of the enterprise, we must capture the actions of both humans and systems. On its face, this sounds like a daunting task: Capturing how groups of people and key individuals interact with one another and with systems could easily consume thousands of staff hours of time in interviewing many people, documenting and collating the results, and developing a model of the resulting data. In addition to the sheer amount of labor this approach would require, it presents several additional problems. First and foremost, people may not accurately remember every action they've taken; every system they've used to process data; and all the data that they've created, reviewed, and updated as part of a specific task. Second, there is the problem of human nature: none of us wants to tell someone else about all the details and problems of their workday because it could cast them or someone else in a bad light, especially if the person made a mistake. And people will certainly be reluctant to advertise deviating from established policy or procedures such as those captured in the process models discussed in Chapter 4. Because one of our goals is to identify deviations between the process models and how the work is actually performed, people's unwillingness to admit to that deviation would present a problem for the enterprise architect.

There is another important reason to avoid using interviews or surveys to capture enterprise behaviors: People have more important things to do with their time. Each person interviewed has a job and a primary purpose in the enterprise, and that purpose is something other than feeding information to the architecture effort. Every person in the enterprise should be working toward achieving the enterprise's goals, and when a person is diverted from their primary tasks to feed the enterprise architecture effort information, that adversely affects the enterprise's progress toward those goals.

In years past, personal interviews were likely the only viable method for capturing behaviors in the enterprise. But today we have more direct and more efficient ways to capture most of the information we need to model behaviors. The emergence of cybersecurity as a major concern in even small enterprises has provided us with new tools that can help us understand what is actually going on: ubiquitous system and application logs. Coupled with the continuous monitoring tools that are used in many enterprises, these logs provide a great deal of the information needed to model the behaviors of both humans and systems.

Application and system logs capture many of the information elements that are important in modeling behaviors. They record each time a user logs in; the information the user accessed, created, or deleted; the connections to other systems and data transferred between them; and other important activities such as software updates and system outages. These logs reveal the core information that we want to model: which systems users are interacting with and the data flow among those systems. This information is the heart of the any behavior model and is critical to our ability to understand how the enterprise is really functioning.

As important as the information captured in log files is, and as inefficient as interviewing people is, log files do not answer all of our questions about enterprise behaviors. At some point, we will have no alternative to interviewing users for learning the details of their behavior. System logs do not capture interactions among individuals such as conversations, planning meetings, and the like. A great deal of an enterprise's activities happen over e-mail, but it is very difficult to make an association between e-mail exchanges and the interactions of users with other systems. For example, an e-mail from a supervisor approving a travel request may not be easily associated with the travel system logs that show a user purchasing tickets and booking a hotel. We will only be able to understand those details by talking to the parties involved.

Just remember that personal interviews are an inefficient means of gathering this information, so do as much as you can to mitigate the problems associated with using interviews to gather information. Do not interview users until you have a set of specific questions to ask them about the particulars of the behavior you are trying to model. Sitting down with someone and asking them to tell you how they do their job will not yield an accurate model for the reasons previously discussed. Avoid asking open-ended questions whenever possible; it is much more effective to ask questions that will lead to specific answers that clarify specific points. For example, asking someone how the travel-request approval process works is very open ended and most of that information could likely just as well be recovered from system logs (e.g., a user might log in and create a travel request, which will later be marked as approved). It would take less time and yield more accurate results to ask a single clarifying question about information that is not available in the logs: Is the person who approves the travel request the one who enters it in the system, or does that approval come from someone else? This is an easy question to answer that will take minimal time for all concerned and clarifies the information already captured in the system logs.

# Documenting Behaviors

Once the information describing the behaviors is captured, we need to transfer it into a format that supports detailed analysis, preferably automated analysis. That is, we need to convert that raw information into a behavior model. While automated analysis will not provide all the answers we may want, the fact that the behavior is formally modeled will ensure that we really understand the structure and details of the behavior and that the ambiguities have been removed from the model as much as possible.

Modeling behaviors is an iterative process; there is no escaping that. The process is iterative because the chances that we can accurately capture all of the factors in the behavior in one pass are exceedingly small. Every time we capture some aspect of a behavior, there is a good chance we will discover some other characteristic of the behavior that is unclear or not quite what we originally thought it was. This sounds like an unending process of refinement that could easily get out of control, but keep in mind that the behavior model only needs to be accurate enough to understand the major factors that produce an effect that either helps or hinders an enterprise in achieving its goals. The key to keeping the behavior-modeling task under control is to start with a relatively simple behavior model that captures the behavior's major activities and to then analyze the model to see if the factors that are producing the effects are accurately captured. The only reason to continue modeling beyond that point is if there are one or more activities whose effects you do not understand. You only need to understand them well enough to determine if they are having effects on achieving the specific goal in question.

Once you have identified the initial set of activities, you will need to assemble them into a model of the behavior you want to analyze. You can capture this model in any of a number of process diagrams, including UML activity models, BPMN models, state machine diagrams, or any other formalization tool you are comfortable using. Whenever possible, you should model the behaviors using the same tool used to document the processes described earlier. Using the same modeling technique will make it easier to compare the expected activities (the process model) with the observed activities (the behavior model), and will also make it easier to relate the behavior model to the enterprise goals (just as the process models are related to enterprise goals).

One of the key tasks in assembling the behavior model will be placing the activities in the correct order. One of the easiest ways to do this is to use the time stamps from the system and application logs (assuming the information was gathered in the log files). This will probably not capture all of the necessary ordering information, but it will at least provide a rough sense of the ordering. An activity recorded at 10:00 a.m. obviously occurred earlier in the behavior than an activity recorded at 11:00 a.m. the same day. That is enough information for a rough ordering with respect to time, but it is not sufficient to construct an accurate behavior model. Without additional information, we cannot tell if there is any dependency between the activities: is the first activity a necessary precondition of the second activity, or are they unrelated activities with no relation between the different times they took place?

Information contained in the system logs may help clarify activity-ordering questions. If the first activity was followed by an information transmission from the first system to the second, then it may be reasonable to infer that there is a dependency. The absence of any information transmission may likewise indicate that there is no significant relationship between the two. This is the kind of information that must be clarified with the actors who participated in the activities or with other knowledgeable parties. It is also possible that there was an information exchange that was not recorded in the logs; this would be a good indication that the logs are not complete enough and should start recording additional information.

A (very) simple example of part of a behavior model is shown in Figure 5-1, which depicts an expansion of the process shown in Figure 4-1. In this case, a review of system logs and interviews with the sales team revealed that monitoring the results of a new advertising campaign is not a single activity conducted by the sales team but rather a distinct series of steps that includes exchanging information with an outside data analysis firm.

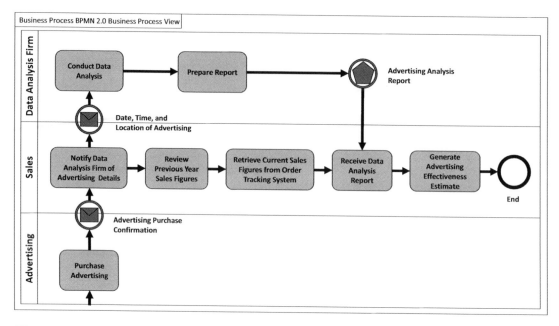

**Figure 5-1.** *Detail of Behavior Model*

As stated, this diagram is very simple, but it serves to illustrate that the activities involved in monitoring the results of an advertising campaign and its effects on sales are more complicated than the enterprise architecture team originally thought. It also reveals some simple emergent behaviors, illustrated by the sales team retrieving the previous year's sales data to ensure it has a valid baseline to compare to the latest sales data. It also reveals that there is an outside consulting company supporting the sales team's efforts to understand the effects of the new advertising campaign with data analysis services.

# Environment

Modeling the environment is not like modeling processes or behaviors. We are not talking about a creating specific, discrete model of the environment. Instead, modeling the environment is akin to modeling data: there are a number of values and specifications that need to be captured for use in the enterprise architecture, and it is helpful to collect them into a coherent group.

The reason for modeling the environment is that there are a large number of factors that are outside the enterprise's control but that nevertheless have an effect on the enterprise's ability to achieve its goals. The enterprise architect must take these factors into account if he or she is going to produce a reasonably accurate model of the enterprise and its systems. There are many factors that go into modeling the environment, but the primary environmental factors the enterprise architect should capture are those affecting how the enterprise deploys and operates its systems. Generally speaking, these are the infrastructure environment the enterprise must operate with. Other environmental factors include external actors and external systems, each of which must be accounted for.

# Infrastructure Environment

The infrastructure the enterprise must operate within includes a number of factors. Physical data centers, infrastructure service providers, available communications bandwidth, and the intended operating environment are the major factors to consider. Data centers owned and operated by the enterprise function in something of a grey area in the enterprise architecture. In one respect, the data center is a part of the enterprise architecture itself, because the enterprise controls the data center and its capabilities and can adjust those as needed to help achieve the enterprise's goals. But the cost of building or updating a data center, including possible regulatory questions such as zoning issues, can effectively make a data center a permanent factor that must be accepted as-is for the immediate purposes of the enterprise architecture.

As cloud computing becomes more pervasive, many enterprises are transitioning from maintaining their own hardware and data centers to outsourcing that infrastructure to cloud service providers such as Amazon Web Services, Microsoft Azure, and others. While commercial cloud providers make available a broad array of useful services for the systems they host, they do impose some restrictions, and those restrictions must be understood and accounted for in the enterprise architecture. In reality, the restrictions are no different in principle from the restrictions that an enterprise had to face when hosting its systems internally, such as specific processor architectures, available bandwidth, and the like. The difference is that by moving to the cloud, the enterprise surrenders control over most of these factors. That does not mean the factors cease to affect the enterprise's systems and its ability to achieve its goals. And because they affect the enterprise's behaviors, they must be accounted for in the enterprise architecture.

A similar environmental factor affects many government systems. In many cases, particularly with the systems developed within the US Department of Defense, a system is developed by one organization but an entirely independent organization is responsible for building and maintaining the communications infrastructure that the system will rely on. The infrastructure provider has its own requirements and goals, and usually has a single infrastructure that supports many different systems and organizations, and thus the desires of any one system developer must be balanced against those of all the other system developers. In effect, such a situation is an enterprise of enterprises, and the architect of any given enterprise must treat the infrastructure provider as an external organization that imposes certain restrictions that must be accepted as a fact of life.

Communications bandwidth must also be considered part of the infrastructure environment. While some enterprises may have the ability to run more cable or improve the wireless communication infrastructure, most of them will be constrained to work with the communications limitations as an immutable factor. This is a particular concern in enterprises that have significant elements deployed to austere environments where the communications infrastructure is either very limited or unreliable. One obvious example is military systems, which are routinely deployed in areas where the only communications infrastructure available is the radio systems the deploying organization brings along with it. These systems must rely on radio frequency communications with very limited throughput. This same issue applies to systems as diverse as mobile electronic commerce systems and telemedicine systems, where the availability of reliable communications may be in question. Each of these systems must be constructed in a way that takes these communication limitations into account so that their effects on the enterprise's ability to achieve its goals can be factored into the understanding of enterprise behaviors.

Many infrastructure factors take the form of restrictions on how systems are deployed and operated. As such, they may be best treated as constraints on the architecture, but understanding that these constraints are external is important when planning how the enterprise can achieve its goal. External constraints are much harder to change than internal constraints; modeling them separately helps the architecture team recognize that status.

# Organizational Environment

The environmental factors that should be modeled include external organizations the enterprise interacts with on a regular basis. These organizations are usually outside the direct control of the enterprise, but they can have a significant effect on the enterprise's ability to achieve its goals and on the behaviors that emerge from the enterprise. As important factors that affect the enterprise, external organizations must be accounted for in the enterprise architecture.

For example, a retail seller will have to deal with external organizations that include suppliers; the public; banks and other financial institutions; government organizations such as state and federal tax authorities; and competitors. All of these organizations may take actions that affect the enterprise's ability to achieve its goals, and they may need to be included as part of process and behavior models. In addition, each of these external organizations may have systems that the enterprise may need to interface with to exchange data or invoke services. If a retailer accepts credit cards, then the credit card transactions must be submitted to an internal processing system that verifies the card is valid, applies the transaction amount to the card holder's bill, and bills the retailer for the transaction processing fee. These are all factors outside the retailer's control, but they do have an effect on the retailer's operations and therefore on the retailer's ability to achieve its enterprise goals.

An external organization is really a special kind of an actor and can be modeled as an actor. But I recommend modeling external actors separately for two main reasons. First, modeling them separately establishes a clear delineation between internal actors and external actors. The enterprise can directly affect internal actors, directing them to take some actions and not take others. Internal actors can be controlled, and they are presumably working to achieve the enterprise's goals (and if they are not, they can be redirected or changed). Some external actors may also be working to help the enterprise achieve its goals; for example, a management consulting company that has been employed to help the enterprise improve efficiency. But most external actors will be either neutral or hostile to the enterprise's goals. The credit card processor may care only that it gets its fee from a retailer; whether the retailer meets its sales goals is of no importance to the processor. In contrast, a competing retailer may be actively working against the enterprise's goals. One retailer increasing market share generally means another retailer loses market share, and the second retailer is unlikely to sit back and let that happen without a fight.

# System Environment

Just as infrastructure and external organizations are part of the enterprise's environment, so are external systems. I will discuss modeling systems in more detail in the next section, but it is appropriate at this point to discuss how external systems are differentiated from internal systems. Both are modeled using the same techniques, but because the enterprise architect cannot direct changes to external systems, their effects on the enterprise's ability to achieve its goals and on the emergence of behaviors within the enterprise must be clearly understood.

Because external systems are completely outside the control of the enterprise architect, the enterprise architect will know almost nothing about them except whatever information is available as part of the interface specification. External systems are really the ultimate black box: an entity whose functions are completely obscured from outside view. In fact, the functions of the external system are usually so completely obscured that the enterprise architect can never really be sure whether an external system is a single system, a collection of related systems, or a combination of systems and human actors completing some function. Those details are completely irrelevant to the enterprise architect; the only factors that matter are understanding the interface, the external system's function with respect to the enterprise, and the fact that the system is external to the enterprise.

Just as external actors are modeled in the same way as internal actors, external systems should generally be modeled in the same way that internal systems are modeled, but they should be grouped as external systems to keep a clear delineation in the enterprise architecture between those things the architecture team can control (internal systems) and those it cannot (external systems). The one primary difference in how external systems are modeled is that the enterprise architecture team will never know anything about their internal structure; it will always remain a large-scale black box. This is in contrast to the models of internal systems, where the system model may be further decomposed into major components at the enterprise level in cases where a specified enterprise goal depends on understanding a certain internal structure.

Most often, the only things the enterprise architect will know about an external system are the details of the interface that is exposed to the enterprise and the service that the system provides (e.g., credit card transaction processing). This information is generally provided on a take-it-or-leave-it basis, and the enterprise can either accept that interface, find another provider of that service, or go without the service entirely. In some cases, it may be possible to negotiate a change to the interface, but this will be the exception rather than the rule. The external organization is probably providing the same service to many consumers and customizing the interface for each consumer would be impractical.

Understanding the interface means understanding the functions the interface makes available, the data the interface consumes for each of those functions, and the data the interface provides for each of those functions. To continue with the example of a credit card transaction processor, we might know that the interface provides three functions: one for validating a credit card, one for completing a credit card purchase, and one for executing a refund to the credit card. The card validation function might require the card holder's name, the card number, the expiration date, and the card verification value (CVV). (The CVV is the three-digit number found on the back of most credit cards.) The data returned by this function may be a simple Boolean value (e.g., "True" if the card is valid). The card purchase function might require all of the same information as that used for the card verification plus the purchase price and some identifier for the seller. It will return a verification code if the transaction is successful or an error code if the transaction fails. This data should be modeled using the same techniques as those for all the other data handled or stored in the enterprise, and it should be clearly associated with those interface functions.

When modeling interfaces provided by external systems, it is important to understand all of the functions available from those interfaces, even if they are not currently in use. Each of these functions is an option the enterprise can use in updating its own systems and may be helpful in achieving one or more of the enterprise's goals. Not knowing that those functions are available leaves a significant hole in the enterprise architect's understanding of the environment the enterprise is operating in.

# Systems

Modeling the systems within the enterprise is what traditional enterprise architecture frameworks focus on, but the approach I describe here considers them secondary models. Keep in mind that by "secondary," I do not mean that they are of less importance; I mean the architect should produce these models later in the process of creating the enterprise architecture. That said, I do consider system modeling a less-important activity in the context of enterprise architecture than other activities.

Traditional enterprise architecture frameworks begin by decomposing high-level requirements and desires into progressively more detailed representations until there is enough detail to specify the individual systems that make up the enterprise. The result of this approach is an enterprise architecture that includes all of the implementation details of the various systems in the enterprise. This is a hangover from the frameworks' heritage; most began life as system architecture frameworks. When it became apparent that there was a need for enterprise architecture, many of the system architecture frameworks were "promoted" and rechristened enterprise architecture frameworks. As discussed earlier in this book, that approach has not scaled well, and it is the primary reason that many managers are coming to see enterprise architecture in general as a failed effort.

I take a very different approach than traditional frameworks to defining systems within the enterprise architecture. I consider the implementation details of individual systems to be beyond the scope of enterprise architecture, and so to be of little interest to the enterprise architect, who should treat them that way. Within the enterprise architecture, the architect should model individual systems as a series of one or more black boxes with defined interfaces. How many black boxes the system model should contain depends on how the system is licensed or implemented. When systems are fielded as a single coherent unit (e.g., a commercial payroll system), the best way to model them is as a black box. When fielding systems that contain a collection of components the enterprise may replace or upgrade individually, the architect should model them in detail.

## Monolithic Systems

Commercial software vendors often create and sell their systems as a monolithic unit that customers buy and field as such. The customer cannot break them up into individual components for reuse in other unrelated systems, and cannot upgrade individual components without an upgrade of the entire system. The same is often true of custom-developed systems. In effect, the architect must treat these systems as a single unit. They will interface with other systems in the enterprise in different ways, but other than that, the enterprise architect cannot modify them.

The enterprise architect should model these systems as individual black boxes with specified interfaces. The commercial vendor defines those interfaces, including their input and output data formats. Despite the fact that these systems are part of the enterprise, when modeling them the architect should treat them in much the same way as external systems. The details of their internal functioning are not visible to the architect; only the externally visible effects are apparent. That is really all that matters to the enterprise architect.

It is important to model the externally visible effects of these systems, together with details of their available interfaces, so that the enterprise architect can understand how they fit into the processes and behaviors of the enterprise. This modeling also gives the enterprise architect the information needed to understand the implications of exchanging such a system with a comparable system from another vendor or with an internally developed system.

Understanding the externally visible effects of the system, combined with its interfaces, makes it possible to predict the effects that removing the system or attempting to replace it will have on the enterprise. If the architecture team decides to remove the system without replacing it, then any process or behavior that relied on those effects must change. Architects can substitute a different system that produces the same effects or actors can alter their workflow to adapt to the loss of the system. Either way, we can expect an effect on the emergent behaviors of the enterprise.

If architects identify a substitute system that has the same effects, then unless it has the same interfaces as the original system, developers need to update every system that interacts with the replaced system to work with the new system. This will require some development work, and it is reasonable to expect some change to any enterprise behaviors that involve the replaced system.

# Component Systems

Some commercial systems, and many custom-developed systems, are collections of independently developed components that developers integrate to form the resulting system. Unlike monolithic systems, developers can often trade out the individual components that make up these systems and replace them with other components that perform the same functions. This is especially easy when the two components have identical interfaces.

The enterprise architect should model these component systems as a set of discrete black boxes connected by well-defined interfaces. Deciding how far each black box should be decomposed is a matter of judgment; rules that work for one component system may not work well for another. A good rule of thumb is that these systems should be decomposed to the level at which the individual components are packaged and made available as coherent units intended to be reused as a unit. Put another way, if a single installation of the component in question can be used by multiple systems, then the architect should model it independently; otherwise, it should not be visible from the enterprise architecture level.

For example, an open-source relational database management system may include a component that takes care of the basic database management functions, a component used to write application logs, and a component that provides a web interface through an application server. The application-logging component may be a commonly used open-source logging utility, but if an external system cannot write events to that logging utility, then the architect should not model it separately. In contrast, if other applications can install their interface components in the application server packaged with the database system, then the architect should model the application server separately from the database management system. In such a case, the model must clearly include the fact that the database management system depends on the application server.

By modeling component systems in this way, the architect gains several advantages. First, by breaking systems down into reusable components, the architect can identify commonly used components across multiple systems. This is a necessary first step in driving the enterprise to increase commonality and interoperability across systems (assuming that is an enterprise goal). If four systems are using the same authentication component but a fifth system is using a different authentication component, that is likely a source of interoperability problems in addition to being an opportunity for increasing commonality by transitioning the fifth system to the common authentication component.

The second advantage is that modeling the individual components and their interfaces provides the information needed to understand when some proposed new component can or cannot take the place of an existing component. If the proposed new component performs the same functions as the existing component and has the same interfaces, then the replacement will be feasible without significant reworking and the architect can focus on other comparison factors. However, if the interfaces are not similar, then the architect knows the proposed replacement will require reworking of other systems or components.

A third benefit to modeling at the component level is that is gives enterprise-level visibility to possible vulnerabilities. When a weakness in a given software package or an interface specification is discovered, it is imperative that the enterprise be able to assess its overall vulnerability to that exploit. Being able to query the enterprise model to identify those components is much more efficient than trying to assess each individual system.

# Standards

Standards are important to the enterprise architect because an enterprise architecture is supposed to help improve interoperability and data sharing among systems in support of the enterprise's goals. However, it is important to understand that not all standards are equal, and standardization for the sake of standardization is often a fool's errand. The enterprise architect thus needs to approach standards with a clear understanding of the enterprise's goals and with a commitment to properly applying standards to the challenge of meeting those goals.

Most of the standards the enterprise architect cares about will be data standards or interface standards. When modeling these standards, there are often existing formal specifications the architect can reuse rather than trying to create new descriptions of the standards by using some other modeling convention. Wherever possible, the easiest way to incorporate standards in the architecture model is to link them to the data exchange or system interface that they were implemented by. In effect, this is capturing the standard as a link to an external reference rather than creating a new model.

Standards are usually associated with systems and their interfaces, in particular with the data formats consumed and produced by those interfaces. However, standards may also be associated with processes or activities, and not with systems. Manually developed work products may have an associated standard in the same way as data generated by a system does. Regardless of what the standard is associated with, the architect must clearly identify what the standard is and how it applies to the architecture. Unless it is clearly linked to the architecture, the appropriate use of a standard will not be clearly understood by the implementation teams who are expected to utilize it.

In practice, standards come in two main forms: de jure standards and de facto standards. The enterprise architecture should handle each of these standards a little differently, but the result should be the same: a well-crafted model of the data and interface formats that supports automating analysis of the enterprise architecture and testing of the enterprise. If one of the goals of the enterprise architecture effort is to increase interoperability among enterprise systems, an effective way to do that is to test interfaces against the standards they are supposed to implement. If the standard is clearly and formally documented, then crafting a test to verify that an interface or a data artifact conforms to the standard is a relatively straightforward activity. That should be the primary goal when modeling standards within an enterprise.

# De Jure Standards

By "de jure" standards, I mean those specifications that have been developed and approved by a standards-setting body such as the International Standards Organization (ISO) or the Institute of Electrical and Electronics Engineers (IEEE). The primary functions of these bodies include developing, reviewing, and approving standards. The standards they publish are accepted across multiple industries, academia, and many governments because they have been thoroughly reviewed and are maintained by dedicated working groups whose members have many years' experience in the field and in developing useful standards.

Examples of de jure standards span functions as diverse as defining the specific alloy content of the structural steel used in bridges, to specifying the waveform of the alternating currents used in household wiring, to standardizing the size and content of packets exchanged among information systems. Most of the standards of interest to the enterprise architect relate to the field of information technology and come from organizations like ISO and IEEE, among others.

Most of the time, standards bodies use some precise notation system to define the standard. For example, the Open Geospatial Consortium's KML[1] specification for expressing geographic information is defined using the XML Schema Definition (XSD). The XSD used by KML defines the KML specification with enough detail to validate any instance of a KML document to ensure the format is correct, and it provides enough information for developers to create conformant implementations. Recreating this specification is a waste of the architect's time and introduces a maintenance problem. Every time the standards body updates the specification, the architect has to update the architecture model. It is much simpler to just link to the authoritative version and leave it at that.

One thing that architects should avoid whenever possible is creating new standards unless there is no other way to solve a specific interoperability problem. Many governments have a tendency to create government-specific standards, whether out of habit or because they believe there are no suitable existing standards. Creating new standards out of habit is a holdover from the days when standardization was much less common, particularly in information technology systems. Back when only governments could afford to build large information systems, interoperability required a government-developed standard because there were no international standards bodies. In many

---

[1]Formerly the Keyhole Markup Language.

cases, that old habit has persisted, and government organizations spend countless hours and large sums of money to develop their own original standards. In most cases, an existing commercial or international standard meets the vast majority of the needs that inspired the government-specific standard in the first place.

In a few cases, a government-developed standard may be appropriate. For example, the symbols used on military operations maps to identify friendly, enemy, and neutral forces are not the sort of thing with a large-enough commercial constituency to interest a dedicated standards body. However, in the vast majority of cases, developing a custom standard is a poor use of limited resources. In most commercial enterprises, there is even less need to develop a specification where no suitable commercial or international standard exists. The fact that there is no standard does not necessarily mean interoperability will be more difficult. De facto standards may be all that developers need.

# De Facto Standards

De facto standards are not "standards" in the formal sense. There is no industry consortium that establishes and maintains them; there is no body of experts that carefully examines every proposed change and decides whether it will be adopted; and there is no publicly visible process for proposing and debating changes. Instead, de facto standards are just those data and interface formats that are so commonly used that they might as well be de jure standards.

Perhaps the most commonly known de facto standard is the Microsoft Word document format. It is widely used in industry, academia, and government despite the fact that it is not the product of a typical standards body. Instead, because Microsoft Word is so widely used, its document file format has become the most common file format used for exchanging word-processing documents. It has emerged as a standard despite the fact that it was developed by a single commercial vendor and not by a consortium of industry representative or academics.

The fact is that most information technology systems rely almost entirely on de facto standards and not on de jure standards. The most important standards underpinning modern information technology systems are those from the Internet Engineering Task Force (IETF). Standards such as transmission-control protocol (TCP), Internet protocol (IP), Ethernet, and many others have been through a thorough review process but no standards organization has ever formally approved them. That is why most IETF publications carry the designation "Request for Comment" (RFC). They are published as just that—a request for comment on a proposal. Those that receive enough community acceptance become de facto standards.

Just because a de facto standard has not been through a process supervised by an international organization does not mean de facto standards are defined less rigorously than de jure standards. A review of any RFC published by the IETF will reveal a meticulously defined description that provides just as much rigor as any publication of an international standards body. This does not mean that all de facto standards are documented as well as formal standards, but many are.

If a de facto standard within your architecture does not include a formal definition, then the enterprise architecture must document it with sufficient detail to support the level of automated analysis it wishes to apply to the enterprise architecture models. Ideally, the architecture team will document each de facto standard as rigorously as it does the de jure standards, but the reality is that this may not be feasible. If there is no good documentation for any given standard, the enterprise architecture should note that fact.

# Summary

The models described in this chapter are models I call "secondary," but they are not secondary in importance; they are only secondary in the order of creation. Each of these models relies on, and is related to, one or more primary models. In spite of the implication of the name, these models form the core of any enterprise architecture.

Behaviors are one of the primary concerns of my approach to enterprise architecture. The behaviors that emerge from any complex system are of the most interest to the enterprise architect. Where the processes described in Chapter 4 represent idealized conceptions of the way an enterprise will conduct its affairs, the behaviors described here represent what actually happens. They reflect those characteristics of how the enterprise performs that have the largest effect on the enterprise's ability to achieve its goals.

Modeling behaviors captures how people actually use systems, how the systems are related to one another, and the tasks the systems perform. Many of these interactions are not readily predictable, so capturing them allows the enterprise architect to compare what the enterprise is doing with how that either contributes to or detracts from the enterprise's ability to achieve its stated goals. The easiest way to create behavior models is to capture the necessary information from system and application logs. These logs represent real-world activities, and most enterprises with an effective cybersecurity-monitoring program will already be gathering this information, reducing the amount of effort required to create the behavior models. In some cases, the logs will not provide sufficient information to capture the behaviors, and the enterprise architect will need to document the models by interviewing users. Regardless of how the information is gathered, the behaviors should be documented using a formal process model to enable automated analysis and comparison to processes, other behaviors, and to other models in the architecture.

Modeling the environment includes modeling factors that affect the enterprise architecture but are generally beyond the control of the enterprise. Such factors include the infrastructure into which the enterprise systems are deployed and in which they are executed. In some cases, infrastructure models may include assets that are owned by the enterprise but are difficult to change due to the cost and schedule required to complete such a change. Other important aspects of the environment include the external organizations that interact with the enterprise being modeled and the external systems that the enterprise uses in the course of achieving its goals. The important thing about modeling the environment is to understand that although these are effectively immutable constraints, these factors may have a significant effect on the enterprise's ability to change and therefore its ability to achieve its goals.

The systems that are internal to the enterprise form another important part of the enterprise architecture but not in the same manner as the traditional architecture frameworks do. Where traditional enterprise architecture frameworks have been focused on producing a detailed understanding of systems' intended function to support development of those systems, the architecture framework discussed here treats individual systems' internal structure and functions as beyond the scope of the enterprise architecture. In this framework, I model systems as black boxes that perform well-understood functions accessed through well-defined interfaces. Some systems are monolithic, and architects or developers cannot readily separate them into individual reusable components. Other systems are composed of a number of separable components, and developers can update individual components and reuse them across systems to improve efficiency and interoperability. Modeling systems to this level of detail helps the enterprise architect find and leverage commonalities among systems.

Standards are another significant part of most enterprise architectures. While some are de jure standards published by a dedicated standards-creating body, others are made up of commonly adopted data and interface definitions that are so commonly used they form de facto standards. While they are not formal standards, the enterprise architect should treat them as if they were. Provided that systems can implement a set of standards and allow them to successfully interoperate, there is no practical difference between de facto and de jure standards. When no existing standard is available, the enterprise architect should avoid the impulse to define enterprise-unique standards; this is almost always more effort than it is worth. Regardless of where the standards come from, it is important to document them with sufficient detail to enable automated analysis of the architecture models as well as automated conformance testing, as conformance is a key element of improving interoperability.

# CHAPTER 6

# Modeling the Enterprise Architecture

Defining the proper scope and concern of enterprise architecture, understanding the difference between models and diagrams, specifying the types of models that should be created—these are all useful things, but they don't tell us much about *how* to model an enterprise architecture. This chapter describes how to combine these elements into a functional, manageable architecture that senior leaders can use to guide the enterprise and make progress toward achieving its goals.

As I explained earlier, traditional enterprise architecture frameworks assumed that the enterprise architect would start from a high-level, very abstract statement of requirements and recursively decompose them until there was enough technical detail to hand it off to an implementation team. This type of top-down control made sense when enterprises were creating single large information systems. However, the people who developed the architecture frameworks in those days were working in the early days of information technology and computer science. Relatively few information systems even existed, and the capabilities of those that did exist were very limited. Each time a new information system was developed, it is highly probable that it was some new kind of capability, one for which there were no existing information systems to serve as templates. Even into the 1990s, many of the IT capabilities we take for granted today did not exist. Development teams had to invent new capabilities every time they implemented a new system.

The situation today is very different. It would be ridiculous to say that every IT capability that can be invented has already been invented, but the vast majority of information systems that are implemented today are either reimplementations of existing systems using more modern technologies or they provide a new capability by assembling existing technologies in a novel way. Most development teams do not have to invent anything; they have plenty of examples to use as templates. This is why a modern

© John D. McDowall 2019
J. D. McDowall, *Complex Enterprise Architecture*, https://doi.org/10.1007/978-1-4842-4306-0_6

approach to enterprise architecture is so very different from the traditional approach: the vast majority of development teams assemble existing components and integrate existing systems to meet users' needs; they do not invent entirely new capabilities.

Yes, there are times that development teams must invent entirely new capabilities. The field of machine learning is one obvious area where researchers are developing new techniques and practitioners are creating new capabilities. Yet those situations are the exception, not the rule. Similarly, the vast majority of enterprise architecture efforts are established to bring a measure of order to the existing conglomeration of systems within an enterprise, not to start from a clean slate and design an architecture for an entirely new enterprise. The approach to enterprise described in this chapter reflects that understanding and takes advantage of it to make the enterprise architecture effort both tractable and effective.

# Dynamic Enterprise Architecture

An enterprise architecture framework is a means of organizing the architect's thoughts and the architecture products, partly to divide them into manageable chunks and partly to ensure that the architecture addresses all of the various concerns such as user experience and infrastructure. But the enterprise architecture itself—the products produced by the architect within the bounds of the framework—has traditionally occupied a role analogous to that of a building architecture. When preparing to erect a building, the architect draws out plans for how the finished structure will look, which include some information about what materials the builder should use. Once the builder has put up the building, the architect's job is complete, and the plans are filed away or disposed of because the architecture has fulfilled its purpose. The architect moves on to other pursuits. The building stands and is used, relatively unchanged, until the owner wishes to perform a major renovation. When undertaking a renovation, the first step is usually to hire an architect and start the design and construction process all over again.

Enterprise architecture is different in that the structure of the enterprise is not static. The modern enterprise is highly dynamic: Teams implement, update, and replace systems on a nearly continuous basis; management may restructure the organization periodically; the enterprise may change its mission or business model; and any number of other changes come and go. Enterprise architecture is an ongoing effort to better align the enterprise's systems, processes, and structure to adapt to these changes. In such an environment, why would we expect the enterprise architecture to be a static set of artifacts? Traditional enterprise architecture frameworks treat the enterprise architecture as a fixed set of models or diagrams that development teams take as the starting point for their work. Given how dynamic the modern enterprise is, there is no reason to expect that a static enterprise architecture will be useful more than a few months after the architecture team documented it.

Another important aspect of architecture that the enterprise architect must accept is that no architecture ever survives contact with the development team. Once the architect hands over the architecture model, the architect moves to the back seat and reality drives events. User requirements change during development, new technology emerges, business needs change, schedules change—the list of potential changes is endless. A good development team responds to those changes quickly. New development models such as Agile and DevOps have emerged to deal with this rapid pace of change. The one constant in all of this is that most times, no one updates the original architecture model to reflect the as-fielded system. This is just as true of enterprise architectures as it is of system architectures.

Given this reality, it makes no sense to devote weeks and months to creating a highly detailed enterprise architecture. If the architecture does not accurately reflect the as-fielded systems in the enterprise, it is useless as a management tool. In order to make an enterprise architecture a useful management tool, we must make the enterprise architecture at least as dynamic as the enterprise itself. Any management tool that requires long update and approval cycles before leaders can use it for operational purposes is unsuited to the modern business landscape. The architect must properly scope an architecture in terms of both the level of detail and time. Bounding the architecture in this way limits the task of the architect to a tractable size, and it defines the boundaries in which the architecture is applicable and useful.

## Bounding by Detail

If beginning an enterprise architecture from a high-level requirements statement and progressively decomposing it into implementation-level detail is impractical, it follows that we must have some means of limiting the amount of detail we include in the architecture. To be blunt about it, we must decide how our models will be wrong. We must have some reasonable means of deciding how much detail is enough for the purposes of an enterprise architecture.

The most obvious means of bounding an architecture is to define the scope of that architecture. In the case of an enterprise architecture, we must decide what constitutes the enterprise we are modeling, both in terms of how broad the enterprise is and how deep the level of detail in the enterprise architecture needs to be to make it effective. Deciding how broad the enterprise is requires that we define the limits of our enterprise. We can determine the appropriate level of detail by deciding whether we intend to create a reference architecture or a solution architecture.

## Defining the Enterprise

*Enterprise* is a relative term. In general, when we discuss enterprise architecture, we are talking about an architecture that encompasses all of an organization. But even that is not a sufficiently clear means of deciding what is and is not within the enterprise. Organizations are not unitary constructs; they are often divided into suborganizations along functional lines. A large corporation is an enterprise, but that corporation may also have multiple divisions, each of which is an enterprise in its own right. For example, General Motors is an enterprise, but it has several subenterprises within it: Chevrolet, Buick, and others. Each of these divisions independently manages its own enterprise. The result is an enterprise of enterprises, each of which may have its own enterprise architecture. However, each of those enterprise architectures should align with the overall enterprise architecture (in this case, that would be the General Motors enterprise architecture).

In order to properly define the scope of the enterprise architecture, the enterprise architect must have clear direction from management that spells out the range of the enterprise architect's responsibility. Because the purpose of the enterprise architecture is to meet the enterprise goals as defined by senior leadership, it is the prerogative of that leadership to define the breadth of the enterprise architecture. Furthermore, it is incumbent upon the leadership of the enterprise to define the relationship between the organization's own enterprise architecture and the enterprise architectures of other organizations. In practical terms, this definition usually includes an outline of funding responsibilities. The enterprise leadership will scope its enterprise architecture to encompass all those things they provide funding for and exclude the things they don't.

Even when senior leadership has clearly defined the scope of the enterprise architecture, it is a good practice for the enterprise architect to anticipate relationships and responsibilities that senior leaders have not clearly defined. Continuing with the example of General Motors, an architect tasked with preparing an enterprise architecture for Chevrolet would be wise to keep in mind that Chevrolet is part of the larger General Motors enterprise. Accordingly, the Chevrolet enterprise architecture team should work with the General Motors enterprise architecture team to ensure that, at the very least, their products do not conflict; ideally the Chevrolet enterprise architecture would link to and be derived from appropriate models in the General Motors enterprise architecture.

Defining the scope of the enterprise establishes the breadth of the architecture. The next task is to establish the depth, or degree of detail, that the enterprise architecture must include. There are a number of different terms used to denote levels of detail in an architecture, but I prefer to limit it to two: *reference architectures* and *solution architectures*.

## Reference Architecture

A reference architecture is one that does not specify the implementation details of the systems within it but merely guides and constrains their definition. As the name implies, an implementation team should treat it as a reference and not as a specific design.

A reference architecture for a system defines the major components of the system in generic terms and the expected connections among those components. Details of each component's capabilities, interface specifications, internal structure, and similar implementation information is beyond the scope of a reference architecture; those details should be left to a solution architecture. The reference architecture for a payroll management system might include a user interface, a server component, and a database, with a specification of the connections between the user interface and the server. Details about those connections should not be included in the reference architecture unless the enterprise has a specific goal of making those interfaces common across all systems. Whether the user interface connects to the server over a network or is a web interface hosted on the server is an implementation decision, and as such it is properly the responsibility of the solution architecture.

In the case of an enterprise architecture, trying to define all the expected components and connections among the various systems and applications in the enterprise is at odds with the philosophy of the enterprise as a complex adaptive system. Furthermore, these definitions would be difficult to maintain over time in an Agile or DevOps environment where development teams are continuously updating systems independently of one another. No sooner might the enterprise architecture team document one set of components and connections than the development teams might change the system architectures, requiring an update to the enterprise architecture.

To be useful, an enterprise architecture should be a strictly limited reference architecture. It should include the models discussed in earlier chapters, with a focus on the things that are necessary to guide and constrain system and application developers in the effort to ensure the results of their work are collectively helping the enterprise achieve its goals. Most of this data will be relatively static and unchanging except for planned periodic updates.

One of the most important things the enterprise architecture should define is one or more controlled vocabularies that implementation teams should use to describe their system functionality, their interfaces, and the data that flows across those interfaces. For example, the enterprise architecture might specify that interfaces are described using a combination of communication protocols and port numbers (e.g., "https over port 8443").

Other important models may provide exact specifications of the processes that the enterprise must follow with enough detail that the implementing systems meet the requirements of the laws, regulations, or policies that prescribe those processes. When constructed in this way, the enterprise architecture is not a blueprint for developers to implement but rather a set of guidelines that system implementers will use to ensure they are working toward achieving the enterprise's goals as they design and implement their systems.

## Solution Architecture

A solution architecture specifies how a specific system (or system of systems) should be constructed and operated. Where a reference architecture provides general guidelines, a solution architecture provides specific instructions. It is the detailed implementation design that explains the internal workings of the system.

The primary goal of the traditional practice of enterprise architecture is the eventual development of a solution architecture. The solution architecture is the result of all the decomposition that the traditional enterprise architecture frameworks advocate. While development teams need that implementation detail, it is beyond the scope of the enterprise architecture and should not be included in it. There should be a clean break between the enterprise architecture and the solution architectures.

There is a one-way relationship between a solution architecture and an enterprise architecture. The enterprise architecture documents the goals of the enterprise, the anticipated processes needed to achieve those goals, the data produced and consumed within the enterprise, the relationships among systems within the enterprise, and the other factors that make up the models described in Chapters 4 and 5. The solution architecture uses the enterprise models as inputs and derives specific system implementations from those models. The solution models must conform to the constraints established in the enterprise architecture, such as using terms from the controlled vocabulary to describe system functions. In that respect, a solution architecture must trace its design elements back to those portions of the enterprise architecture from which it was derived by the implementation team.

The reverse is not true: The enterprise architecture does not specify which individual systems implement a given function. That would be too much detail, and would defeat the goal of treating the enterprise as a complex adaptive system. In other words, the enterprise architect is not concerned with how any given business process is implemented provided the enterprise is meeting its stated goals. Whether the process uses a collection of three different automated information systems or an efficient team of seven human beings is irrelevant to the enterprise architect or senior enterprise leadership; their concern is achieving the enterprise's goals. The details of process implementation is highly relevant to the lower-level managers responsible for implementing the processes to achieve those goals. These managers are the ones who must improve efficiency, lower costs, and take other actions to achieve enterprise goals, and so they are in the best position to deal with implementation details.

By trying to decompose from the enterprise level all the way to the solution architecture details, traditional enterprise architecture frameworks have gotten bogged down in too much detail and lost the focus on their primary purpose. Modern development techniques, combined with the increased agility that businesses need to survive in today's dynamic marketplace, make such top-down control impractical. Traditional enterprise architecture frameworks are still useful for developing solution architectures, but they are unsuited to the needs of modern enterprise architecture and the enterprise architect must remain keenly aware of that distinction.

# Bounding by Time

One of the flawed assumptions of traditional enterprise architecture frameworks is that an architecture is an enduring artifact. In practice, all architecture is ephemeral. Where a properly constructed reference architecture may endure for some notable time (perhaps as long as a year), any other architecture should be treated as a transient artifact with limited long-term utility.

An architecture is a fundamentally temporal artifact. Whether it is an enterprise architecture or solution architecture, it will describe one of two periods. The architecture will either reflect some desired end state of the enterprise or system (an objective or "to-be" architecture) or reflect the current state of the enterprise or system (an "as-is" architecture). Anything else is unimportant and potentially misleading.

Every architecture artifact must include a reference to the time the architect created it and the intended purpose of the architecture. A to-be architecture should have some planned future that it represents, and an as-is architecture should have some defined instant in time it reflects. Any architecture artifact without some statement of the time that it represents is of almost no use as a management tool for directing the enterprise because there is no way to tell if it is currently accurate.

## As-Is Architecture

An as-is architecture is an utterly ephemeral product. The validity of an as-is architecture is limited by the ability of an architect or developer to accurately document the current state of an enterprise or system as it is currently operating. In addition, the as-is architecture potentially becomes inaccurate the moment a configuration change or system patch is applied. Outside the limited realm of systems built using model-driven architecture or other methodologies for automatically generating source code from a model, you cannot rely on the original design as an accurate reflection of the system or enterprise as it exists in the present.

The reality of system implementation is that no architecture survives contact with the development team. Even the most carefully considered designs face unexpected difficulties during implementation. Components built to the same standard do not interoperate as expected, user requirements change, or some other factor upsets the carefully laid plans of the architect, and the development team changes the implementation to adapt. In the vast majority of cases, few developers update the architecture from the as-designed state to reflect the as-built system. Even if the development team updates the architecture to reflect the system as built, postfielding system updates will result in a functioning system that differs from the documentation in significant ways.

The most obvious way that a fielded system will differ from the designed system is through software updates. System administrators may update an individual component or a number of interrelated components at the same time. The result is usually a system with different capabilities (and potentially different vulnerabilities) than the ones in the original system design. Even a configuration change, such as switching the authentication mechanism from a local username-and-password pair to a central credential management system, will affect how the system functions and potentially whether and how it helps the enterprise achieve its goals. The systems within the enterprise are in a continual state of flux, and the state of the enterprise today will not necessarily be the state of the enterprise tomorrow, or next week, or next month.

If every system in the enterprise is constantly changing, it would seem that the task of updating as-is architectures is insurmountable. In years past, it would have been a daunting challenge requiring a sizable dedicated staff of modelers. However, the sophisticated cyberthreats that have emerged over the past few years offer an unexpected source of help that can alleviate this burden. Commercial cybermonitoring software does a remarkable job profiling, inventorying, and documenting system configurations as part of the effort to detect unauthorized modifications. The enterprise architect can reuse this information to generate a snapshot of a system at any given time.

Application log and system log analysis tools provide the architect with valuable insight into how actors are using systems within the enterprise, and provide a record of how data moves among systems as well as into and out of the enterprise. This provides a depiction of how the system is actually used, as opposed to how it was designed to be used. For example, corporate travel systems are often designed for a workflow where an employee creates a travel itinerary that must be approved by that person's manager; some systems have a feature where employees may delegate authority to create their itinerary to an executive assistant. In practice, managers may also delegate their approval authority to their executive assistants. Regardless of how the system was designed to function, this is how it is being used.

By combining the system snapshots with data flow information from log files, the architect can create an accurate picture of how the enterprise is functioning at a moment in time. Aggregating several of these snapshots taken at different times reveals some of the emergent behaviors of the enterprise and shows trends and patterns of activity across the enterprise.

## To-Be Architecture

A to-be architecture has a longer shelf life than an as-is architecture, but it is still an artifact with a limited lifespan. The purpose of the to-be architecture is to describe the intended future state of the enterprise. The enterprise architecture team and senior management use this description to develop a plan that aims to transform the enterprise from its current state into the future state. To give the transition plan the best chance of succeeding, the architecture team should base the to-be architecture on a reasonably accurate understanding of the current state of the as-is architecture.

Because the enterprise and the systems within it are in a constant state of flux, the to-be architecture and its associated transition plan are only valid for a relatively short period. The to-be architecture must be a living artifact, updated as the enterprise updates systems and enterprise goals. Furthermore, the architecture team must update the to-be architecture as new behaviors emerge in the enterprise and as old behaviors evolve.

The plan to get the enterprise from its current state to the state described by the to-be architecture usually involves updating existing systems or creating new systems. That means development teams will be creating new solution architectures. Because those solution architectures will not survive contact with the developers, it will be necessary to create new as-is and to-be architectures after implementation teams have completed the system updates. In a DevOps environment, the changes will be even more frequent and regularly updating as-is and to-be architectures will be even more important.

A to-be architecture is a moving target, and the architecture team must update it regularly to ensure the architecture remains relevant to the enterprise. An architecture may express the enterprise's intended state three years in the future, but that three-year period has an end date. If the objective architecture created in 2014 describes the intended state of the enterprise in 2017, that architecture is no longer an objective architecture in 2018. At best, it is a historical artifact. Ideally, the enterprise will have achieved the goals that the architecture represents. If not, then leadership needs to update the enterprise goals and the enterprise architecture team needs to update the to-be architecture to reflect planned changes based on the current situation.

# Creating Models

Now that we have defined the models that should make up an enterprise architecture and the need to properly scope your architecture, we have the necessary context to discuss the real meat of enterprise architecture: creating architecture models. The mechanics of creating the models is not difficult, though it does require attention to detail and a thorough understanding of the selected modeling language. It also requires the architect to put some thought into structuring the architecture, including how large or small individual models will be and how they will be grouped.

Regardless of the modeling language or tool that you select, it is important that you link the different models to each other where they overlap. For example, when you have a model of a system and its interfaces and a model of the data each of those interfaces produces or consumes, the model of the system should include a direct link from each relevant interface to the corresponding data model. In the same fashion, a process or behavior model should include explicit links between activities in those models, the actors who perform those activities, and the systems that those actors use. This linking is critical to enable enterprise-scale analysis of the architecture. Only by linking related models will you be able to analyze the impact of a potential change on the enterprise. If you do not link your architecture models, then you have no way of knowing which processes will be affected by a change in a given system, or which systems may require an update if a data format changes.

You will have to develop many of your models manually because there is no other way to generate them than to have a human create them. Enterprise goals, processes, and data models are all examples of models that you may have to create as part of developing an enterprise architecture. External organizations may develop and maintain some of these models, especially models of standardized data formats, but they are still manually developed models for our purposes. These are the models you create and link together to form your architecture. Taken together, these manual models will form the backbone of your enterprise architecture. However, there are also additional models that put muscles onto the basic skeleton and make your enterprise architecture a valuable management tool.

It is possible for the architect to manually create models that describe the emergent behaviors in the enterprise. But just because something is possible does not mean it is advisable; it may not even be practical. A key characteristic of emergent behaviors is that they arise spontaneously, making it difficult to predict where and how they will arise and what parts of the enterprise will be involved. Instead of trying to capture behaviors manually, it would be much better if we could capture those behaviors automatically. The same cybermonitoring systems that we can leverage to generate the as-is architecture can reveal the emergent behaviors of the enterprise as well. By capturing the actions of actors and the data exchanges among systems, we can capture those emergent behaviors with enough detail to generate an accurate model of the behaviors. Depending on the size of the enterprise and the amount of monitoring information you gather, you may find it useful to create small applications that will convert the output of the cybertools into your selected modeling language or into a format that your modeling tool can import. This will significantly reduce the amount of work it takes to build an accurate behavior model.

Creating behavior models in this way may sound like a daunting task at first, but there are two things to keep in mind about these models. First, you do not need to model *every* emergent behavior in the enterprise. You only need to model those emergent behaviors that relate to the enterprise's goals. Ideally, most of these behaviors will positively contribute to the enterprise's goals, but some behaviors may detract from them. Either way, the behaviors you choose should interest the enterprise architecture team and senior leadership; other behaviors are less important and should have a lower priority. Second, remember that your behavior models do not need to be perfect; they only need to be accurate enough to understand whether the enterprise is making progress toward achieving its goals. Recall from earlier chapters that all models are wrong. Your behavior models only need to be correct enough to suit their purpose; additional detail is irrelevant.

# Modeling Languages

Before you can create a model, you must select a modeling language. That much is obvious; what is not obvious is which modeling language to choose from the many available. An exhaustive discussion of the available modeling languages is beyond the scope of this book, but a brief review of the most common modeling languages will be helpful. There are some modeling languages that are either unique to a specific tool or are designed to support a specific architecture framework. These languages may be usable for your enterprise architecture, but before you select one of them make sure you fully understand the limitations and can live with them. In the discussion that follows, I limit my remarks to languages that are tool- and framework-independent.

A modeling language is a tool, nothing more and nothing less. A modeling language is just as much a tool to the architect as a hammer is a tool to the carpenter or a wrench is a tool to an auto mechanic. Like physical tools, modeling languages are specialized, and any modeling language is more suited to some modeling tasks than others. Despite what vendors and language developers may claim, no one language is suitable for all modeling tasks. There are no silver bullets. Even if there were a silver bullet solution, any child can tell you that silver bullets only work against werewolves; you must fight vampires and other monsters with different tools.

As you read about the modeling languages in the paragraphs that follow, keep in mind the discussion from earlier chapters that a model is a formal specification. There is nothing in that definition about a specific language. You can create a model using any formalism that works for the task you need to accomplish. If you are so inclined, you can create an architecture model as a computer program using a language such as C, Java, Python, or any other Turing-complete programming language. After all, they are formal representations. Most of the time, you will find it much easier to use graphical-modeling languages that were designed for modeling systems and architectures, but do not hesitate to use other languages when they are better suited to your modeling needs.

In practice, you will likely get your best results by using a combination of languages. Most modern modeling tools support more than one language, either natively or through add-on modules. Each modeling language has its strengths and weaknesses, and each is better suited to creating some models than others. In the sections that follow, I give a brief overview of some of the more common modeling languages together with some thoughts on where they are best used in developing a useful architecture.

## Unified Modeling Language

The UML originated as a means for software developers to express their designs in a common graphical format, and its primary use is still in software development. It includes elements common to designing object-oriented software, including classes, interfaces, parameters, use cases, and the like. UML is a standardized language, published and managed by the Object Management Group (OMG), an international technology standards consortium. Over the years, OMG has updated UML to adapt to changing software development practices, but it is still fundamentally a software-modeling language.

An architect can use UML to create any of the models needed for a complete enterprise architecture, but UML's software design heritage may result in some cases where the model is not as precise as you would like. Because UML is a formal language, with well-defined syntax and semantics, UML does support automated analysis of models defined in UML. However, because UML is defined as a graphical language, any support for automated UML analysis is a feature of the modeling tool and is usually not separable into a stand-alone utility. Creating a custom tool to do UML analysis is a significant undertaking and will require the enterprise to devote significant resources to the task. There is an XML representation of UML, the XML Metadata Interchange (XMI) format published by OMG. However, XMI is designed to support the exchange of UML diagrams across modeling tools, and its focus is on the graphical representation of the model more than the structure; it is not easy to use for automated analysis.

Standard UML elements like classes and interfaces are very suitable for modeling systems and interfaces (that is what they were designed for), but I find the language less suitable for modeling systems-of-systems, data, and processes. The liberal use of stereotypes to create tailored UML profiles helps when modeling systems-of-systems and data, but I find the UML Activity model is not well suited to modeling processes and behaviors.

You can use UML Activity models to model processes and behaviors, but the resulting model is likely to contain ambiguities in the process that you will need to clarify in some other way. In particular, UML Activity models have limited support for the details of decision points and for defining the creation or consumption of data artifacts from activities in the process.

UML is very suitable for modeling actors, systems, and aspects of the environment. When modeling processes and behaviors, I prefer to use a language with better support for describing decision points, as well as good support for describing data artifacts that are used in the process.

## Systems Modeling Language

Like UML, SysML is a product of the Object Management Group. SysML is not a distinct language from UML; it is a profile of UML. That is, it reuses parts of UML, modifies other parts of the language, and extends UML to create some new elements. As its name implies, OMG designed SysML for modeling general systems (as opposed to UML's focus on modeling software systems), and it includes elements that are well suited to modeling physical and cyber-physical systems. OMG conceived SysML as a language to support the practice of model-based systems engineering (MBSE). MBSE is an engineering discipline where the focus is on developing detailed models that can be subject to automated analysis for completeness and correctness before implementation teams build the system.

Because it has a broader scope than UML, SysML is better suited for most enterprise architecture models. In particular, SysML includes a type of model called a Parametric model. Parametric models allow the modeler to define constraints on systems and interfaces and to check conformance of the model to those constraints. A good modeler can do the same thing with standard UML, but it requires the modeler to create a highly detailed UML profile that amounts to a re-implementation of SysML.

One of the motivating factors in creating SysML was the ability to run automated analysis of a model to ensure conformance to constraints and other factors. As a result, SysML modeling tools usually support automated analysis of SysML models. However, that support is generally a feature of the modeling tool, and not usable as a stand-alone module. Like UML, SysML is defined as a graphical language, so creating a custom analysis tool is not a trivial undertaking. XMI can also be used to represent SysML, so it is portable across tools.

Its UML heritage gives SysML some of the same strengths and weaknesses as UML. This is especially true when modeling processes and behaviors. SysML does not appreciably extend the UML activity model, and so it suffers from the same ambiguities as UML in that regard. For modeling processes and behaviors, I prefer the Business Process Model and Notation (BPMN).

## Business Process Model and Notation

The BPMN language is another graphical modeling language published and maintained by OMG. Unlike UML and SysML, BPMN is not a general-purpose modeling language; it is a language designed specifically to model workflows and nothing else. BPMN has its roots in the business process engineering field, and it is poorly suited to modeling anything that is not a process. However, specialized languages have their place in modeling and you should use them where they are appropriate.

The initial version of BPMN was a purely graphical language, similar to UML and SysML in that respect. Many modeling tools include utilities that can analyze BPMN models. The publication of BPMN version 2 in 2011 included a formal XML syntax for representing BPMN in a machine-interpretable format. BPMN representation of XML is much less complex than XMI, with less of a focus on graphical representation. The result is a more compact XML representation that focuses on the model's structure instead of its appearance. This makes it easier to create stand-alone custom analysis tools if you need them.

I prefer using BPMN to model processes and behaviors because it has a much richer set of elements for representing workflows than UML or SysML Activity diagrams. In addition to including a robust set of elements for depicting message exchanges, document creation and consumption, and other data artifacts, BPMN includes sophisticated decision point representations than can accurately describe an arbitrarily complex process if you need that level of fidelity in your model.

Many tools that support UML or SysML also support BPMN, and combining the two model types into the same architecture is usually simple. Most tools that support multiple modeling languages also include the means for linking elements of models created in different languages. For example, an activity in a BPMN model can include a link to the UML model of the system that performs that activity. However, a good modeling tool will not let you mix and match model elements from different languages in the same model; doing so would violate the rules of both modeling languages. For example, while you can link from a BPMN activity to a UML system model, you cannot use elements of a UML Activity diagram in your BPMN model.

## Web Ontology Language

Most architects would not consider OWL an architecture modeling language, but I have found that OWL is very useful when modeling enterprise architectures. I use OWL for two primary purposes: modeling data and describing my architecture metamodel.

OWL is a derivative of the Resource Description Framework (RDF), a means for describing data and data models.[1] OWL uses RDF to encode a form of Description Logics, a family of knowledge representation languages developed to support machine reasoning. OWL has the means to define classes of things, the properties of those classes, and the relationships among classes. The primary use of OWL is to define the semantics of the objects it models, making OWL an excellent choice for defining data models. In order to analyze data, we must understand both the syntax and semantics of each element within it; this is true regardless of whether humans or machines conduct the analysis. Without this understanding, the analyst might misunderstand the data. By formally defining the data model using OWL, you can ensure that anyone, whether human or machine, can understand what each data element describes and how those elements relate to one another. Note that this does not mean any system has to store the data that way; systems just need to link their data storage formats to the OWL model.

In addition to modeling data, OWL is an excellent choice for describing your architecture metamodel. Technically, the architecture language you select will defines your language metamodel. Beyond that, you will most likely adopt certain modeling conventions for your architecture, such as using specific stereotypes for model elements,

---

[1]This a grossly simplified description of RDF, but a more detailed description is beyond the scope of this book. For more information, see the RDF specification at www.w3.org/TR/rdf11-concepts/.

or naming conventions for relationships among elements. This helps keep your own enterprise model consistent, and provides a controlled vocabulary for system implementation teams to reuse in describing their system designs. By linking their models to the controlled vocabulary, system implementation teams will minimize miscommunication with the enterprise team and with each other. For example, if one team uses the stereotype "external interface" to describe any interface that its system exposes to other systems, and another team uses "external interface" to describe interfaces provided by other systems, there will be confusion when trying to discuss interfaces. Defining a separate controlled vocabulary that implementation teams align with will minimize this kind of confusion.

It is also possible to use OWL for other enterprise architecture modeling tasks. I have used it to define an enterprise model that captures the details of fielded systems as reported by cybermonitoring tools and links that information to the enterprise architecture originally defined using UML. I exported the UML model from the original modeling tool and converted it into OWL, then imported the data harvested from the cybermonitoring tools. The result was a comprehensive enterprise model that links the as-is and reference architecture elements, yielding an accurate picture of the current state of the enterprise. Because I defined the architecture in OWL, those who use standard off-the-shelf machine reasoning engines can evaluate the entire model for consistency with the reference architecture in a few seconds. This configuration also makes it simple to identify how many instances of a given software package are deployed in the enterprise, how many systems expose a web interface, and complete other portfolio management tasks.

# Modeling Tools

In addition to selecting a modeling language, you will also have to select a modeling tool. Trying to create a formal architecture model by hand would be extremely difficult in any language, especially for graphical languages such as UML and SysML. Whether you select a modeling language and then choose a tool that supports that language or you select a tool and then choose a language supported by that tool is not important. What matters is that you select a formal language and a tool that supports it.

For the most part, commercial modeling tools all have the same level of support for a given language. All tools that support SysML support the full SysML specification. Where tools differ is in their ease of use and in their extra features. Some include utilities that make it easy to create customized profiles of your selected modeling language, and others require that you write out your profile using a text a notation such as XML. Some tools include advanced analysis capabilities such as the ability to run a simulation of a system design. While an enterprise architecture should not include enough detail of individual systems to make the model executable, the enterprise may want to adopt a common tool for use by all architecture efforts. In that case, support for simulations may be an important consideration when selecting a modeling tool.

In addition to commercial modeling tools, there are a number of open-source modeling tools available. Like their commercial counterparts, many open-source tools have good support for their selected languages, differentiating themselves based on other features. In addition, like many other open-source software initiatives, modeling tools vary in their level of maturity and the completeness of their feature set. I have used a number of open-source modeling tools with good results, and many of them have great features.

Regardless of which modeling tool you select, it is advisable to choose one that fully supports both your selected modeling language and an industry standard model import and export format. The most common model interchange standard is XMI, which supports UML and SysML. Other model interchange formats are also available. For example, tools that support the Department of Defense Architecture Framework (DoDAF) and Ministry of Defense Architecture Framework (MoDAF) usually support the Physical Exchange Specification (PES) defined as part of the Unified Profile for DoDAF and MoDAF (UPDM). Selecting a modeling tool that supports a commonly used model interchange format will give you the flexibility to change modeling tools without having to rebuild all your models from scratch.

# Model Sizing

After you've selected a modeling language and a modeling tool, you will face some practical considerations. One of the key considerations is how big to make your models. Except when you are modeling a very small enterprise, modeling your enterprise as a single, all-encompassing model will result in a large, unwieldy model that is difficult to maintain. Such a model will also make it difficult to spread work out among different members of the enterprise architecture team because most tools have trouble with multiple people concurrently editing a single model. Dividing the enterprise architecture into a number of smaller models alleviates this problem while also giving you an opportunity to organize the information in the model and make it easier to find things.

Dividing the architecture into multiple models does not mean dividing it across multiple files or multiple data repositories. That type of division would make it difficult to keep the links among the different models consistent. Dividing the enterprise architecture means creating multiple, linked models within the same enterprise architecture repository. The end result is a "model of models" where no one model depicts everything in the enterprise architecture, but different combinations of models represent different aspects of the architecture with sufficient detail to enable sound decision-making.

Traditional architecture frameworks divide models up into groupings centered on describing individual aspects of the architecture. These groups of models are termed "viewpoints," "perspectives," or a similar descriptive term. There is nothing wrong with thinking of your enterprise architecture along these lines, but you should not feel bound by such a conception of how to divide the architecture. You can just as easily divide your model up along business lines (sales, manufacturing, etc.). In reality, you will probably need a number of different representations to meet the needs of different stakeholders. Senior managers will want to see different groupings and details than integration engineers or system administrators.

Dividing your model up into smaller, more manageable models helps with both the maintainability of the model and the ability to customize views. Trimming down one large model to generate a custom view usually requires more work than combining a few smaller, carefully selected models into a larger view. Incidentally, this is another good reason to use models instead of diagrams for your architecture. Combining a number of pictures to create a single large picture involves a lot of manual work trying to include all of the elements from the original pictures and ensure nothing has been forgotten. Retrieving this information from a model can be done with a simple query, and most modeling tools will allow you to lay out a diagram that accurately depicts the model elements.

Still, this tells you very little about how big to make each model. As with so much else in enterprise architecture, the decision will primarily be a matter of judgment. My advice is to keep your models as small as possible while also keeping closely related items in the same model. You do not want a model to include several hundred elements if you can sensibly divide it into coherent modules of a couple dozen elements each. On the other hand, you do not want to keep track of hundreds of models that each have only a few elements.

A good approach would be to divide the data model into logical components—product specifications, ordering and fulfillment, or some other grouping that fits well with your business domain—instead of using a single all-encompassing data model. The ontology you created to model your enterprise data dictionary maintains links among the data elements. You can establish links among other types of models in a similar fashion. The size of each module and its contents will vary from enterprise to enterprise, and different modeling tools will have different utilities that can help decide how to divide your models.

# Change Control

One of the most important considerations you will face in managing an enterprise architecture is managing change control. The difficulty of this task varies directly with the number of people on the enterprise architecture team and with the number of people using the enterprise architecture. When there are many people on the team, the chance of making conflicting changes increases significantly, and the more people there are who use the architecture, the more people there will be who want to change the architecture to make their own tasks easier. A proper version control system, with regular backups, is an essential feature of any code development system, and your architecture is really just a form of source code.

Most good modeling tools will have some means of change control, especially if they allow concurrent editing of the same model. For example, some tools require an architect to lock a model before making changes, ensuring that two people can't make changes in the same model at the same time. Other tools use a version control system such as Git, where users have to check out the architecture before making any changes, and the person making the changes has to check the architecture back in before anyone else can see those changes.

While tool support for change management is a desirable feature, do not rely on those tool features as your primary means of change control. These features prevent accidental changes to the architecture; they do not ensure changes have been thought out and properly vetted with all stakeholders. There is no substitute for a formal change management process.

A formal change management process does not need to be a heavyweight, meeting-intensive affair. What it does need to be is documented and published, so that all stakeholders understand how to propose changes to the architecture, how the architecture team evaluates those changes, and who makes the decision about which changes are accepted and which are not. One of the easiest ways to manage architecture changes is through the type of defect reporting process used by many system development efforts. There are a number of commercial and open-source change management tools available, and most support some level of workflow customization that allows you to tailor the tool to fit the needs of your enterprise. Tools like this make it feasible to manage the entire change control process with the tool, eliminating the need for meetings to discuss proposed changes. You can still hold such meetings, and meeting in person may help keep emotions from running too high when the architecture team rejects a proposed change. It is also worth keeping in mind that on large products, meeting in person to collaborate on proposed changes often helps ensure all impacts of the proposed change have been considered.

Regardless of whether you use a change management tool or a simple spreadsheet and whether you discuss proposed changes over e-mail or in person, it is important that you keep a written record of the changes. A written record of proposals for changes and their disposition can be invaluable when trying to determine the reason the architecture has evolved into its current form, and a formal change control process helps ensure that the evolution is carefully considered. Your enterprise architecture will change, but it should not undergo frequent radical changes. It is up to you to manage the rate of architecture change in a way that gives system implementers and the enterprise at large time to adapt.

# Summary

One of the reasons the practice of enterprise architecture needs to change is because the practice of system development has changed radically over the past 30 years. As recently as 15 years ago, developing a new system meant creating libraries and utilities from scratch because they were based on new technology or the algorithms they used were not yet well established. Today, most of the components needed to implement a new system are available from a number of prepackaged libraries or commercial tools. There is very little that a developer needs to design from the ground up, and so there is rarely a need for an enterprise architecture that starts from a very abstract level and decomposes to implementation-level detail.

The enterprise is a constantly evolving ecosystem where systems change independently of each other, business needs change regularly, and people discover new and more efficient ways of completing their tasks. That is, the enterprise is a complex adaptive system. Trying to model any dynamic enterprise from the top down is a losing proposition; the enterprise will change faster than the architects can update their models.

We can combat this by treating architecture as an ephemeral thing. The enterprise architect should establish a simple reference architecture consisting of those elements that should endure for a year or more: controlled vocabularies, process models describing legally mandated tasks, and similarly stable artifacts. The architect should create other artifacts as needed for a specific purpose, use them for that purpose, and discard them afterward.

The architect should develop an objective or "to-be" architecture as a means to solve a specific enterprise problem; for example, when the timekeeping system cannot interface with the payroll system. That to-be architecture should be based on the most recent as-is architecture possible, and the best way to capture the as-is architecture is to look at the structure and configuration of systems as they exist on the network. In most enterprises, the same tools used to protect against cyberthreats produce the data needed to generate an accurate, up-to-date picture of the as-is architecture. Once the enterprise architect has decided on what changes to make to solve a current problem, the architect can discard those architectures. When it is time to solve the next problem, the architect can create a new as-is architecture and a new to-be architecture that depicts the changes that will solve the problem.

Regardless of how the architecture team creates models, it must document them using a formal modeling language to support automated analysis and consistency checking. There are many such languages available, including UML, SysML, and BPMN. When selecting a language, the architect should choose one that is framework-independent to ensure that the architecture team has enough flexibility to model the enterprise according to the enterprise's needs and not the tool developer's preconceptions. The architect should also consider using specialized modeling languages such as OWL to create supporting models such as data dictionaries.

Selecting a modeling language is not enough; the architect must also have an adequate modeling tool. Documenting an architecture in a formal language without the help of a tool is nearly impossible. Most commercial and open-source tools support an array of common modeling languages, and most include analysis utilities that help the architecture team get the most use out of the detailed models they have created. Different tools have different features. When choosing a tool, it is important to ensure the tool supports a standardized model import-and-export format to facilitate sharing the architecture with development teams and to prevent vendor lock-in.

Creating a single, all-encompassing architecture model will yield an artifact that is too large for anyone outside the architecture team to understand and analyze. It is best to break up the architecture into smaller models that link to one another. This will keep individual models at a manageable size while still enabling analysis of the entire architecture. Controlling changes to each model and to the entire architecture is vital to ensuring the consistency and predictability of the architecture.

# CHAPTER 7

# Measuring Effects

In previous chapters, I emphasized the need to transform enterprise architecture from a collection of static documents and diagrams into an operational tool that senior leadership can use to steer the enterprise toward achieving its goals. Until this point, we have discussed the need to clearly define the enterprise architecture and document it using formal models, but that does not automatically make your architecture a usable management tool. To make the architecture a real tool, you must be able to measure its effects on the enterprise. If you cannot measure the effects, you have no way of knowing if any of your actions have had any impact on the enterprise. The key to measuring those effects is monitoring your enterprise and comparing it to your architecture.

All enterprises do some form of monitoring already. For example, every business tracks sales, revenues, profits, and other financial metrics. Sales figures are an obvious indicator of whether the enterprise is meeting that goal of increasing overall sales, but financial metrics tell managers almost nothing about the effectiveness of the enterprise architecture effort. They don't reveal anything about other goals such as the security of enterprise systems against outside intrusion, whether systems conform to enterprise policies, whether system development teams are conforming to the enterprise reference architecture, or a host of other metrics of interest to senior leadership. To truly understand the enterprise requires a more thorough monitoring capability.

The important elements of an enterprise monitoring capability can be inferred from the enterprise goals; that is why defining enterprise goals is the first thing I discussed as part of this architecture framework, and why I emphasized establishing measurable goals. The metrics defined for each of those measurable goals determine what kind of monitoring capability the enterprise needs to measure progress toward the goals.

Monitoring system implementation efforts for things like conformance to enterprise architecture constraints (e.g., using the established controlled vocabularies to describe system functions) is comparatively easy. The models developed by the implementation teams can be compared to enterprise architecture models

127

© John D. McDowall 2019
J. D. McDowall, *Complex Enterprise Architecture*, https://doi.org/10.1007/978-1-4842-4306-0_7

and checked for compliance; the fact that both are defined as models makes this comparison easy. Monitoring the operation of the enterprise and its systems is a more complicated effort, and requires observing systems and business processes at run time, capturing the relevant metrics from that observation, and comparing those metrics to the enterprise goals.

At first blush, this may sound like a complicated undertaking. But this is where the work you put into defining architecture models pays its dividends, in that having captured the architecture as formal models makes it easy to compare the planned state of the enterprise (i.e., the architecture) to the actual state of the enterprise (i.e., the emergent behaviors) once you devise the appropriate metrics. Comparing those metrics to the architecture models is a straightforward data analysis task. The trick is in capturing the right metrics. I learned this after a number of years working on a project where we tried to assess the state of the enterprise by comparing the architecture artifacts of individual systems to one another and to the reference architecture in an effort to understand what data different systems stored. The data analysis task took three senior engineers inlcuding myself over six weeks, and that was just to understand a carefully selected subset of mission activities. We later modified our process to define the reference architecture using an OWL model, then captured the data flows into and out of individual systems. Identifying the data stored in a system became a straightforward matter of querying the models to see what data was flowing out of each system. Instead of weeks of senior engineers' time, we completed the task in a matter of minutes.

Put aside any thoughts you have of gathering metrics through a manual process. Asking groups to report on their activities distracts them from performing those activities, and asking implementation teams to report on their activities likewise diverts resources away from their primary purpose and into a secondary activity. Recall that the purpose of an enterprise architecture effort is to help the enterprise achieve its business goals. An enterprise architecture effort that imposes burdensome reporting requirements on the rest of the enterprise is diverting resources away from the enterprise goals. More importantly, manual reporting is often inaccurate and incomplete. Basing important decisions on inaccurate data is not a good idea if you can get more accurate data in a reasonable amount of time.

If you wish to gather metrics about an enterprise without imposing a new burden, some means of automated metrics gathering is the obvious answer. Developing a dedicated enterprise monitoring capability just for the enterprise architecture effort would be a significant undertaking, and would introduce additional costs and tasks that may be unnecessary. However, most large enterprises are already gathering much of the information they need to understand how the enterprise is behaving. This information can often be leveraged to help understand how the enterprise is progressing toward achieving its goals.

The increasing threat posed by cybercriminals compels every enterprise to be more aware of how its systems are behaving. This has led to the development of a robust market in continuous monitoring and reporting tools designed to help the enterprise identify what systems and software are on its network, the data that is flowing into and out of each system, how users are behaving, and other important indicators of unusual activity that might indicate the enterprise has suffered a security breach or is under cyberattack. While this monitoring is intended to help system and network administrators defend against cyberthreats, it can also be used to help the enterprise's leadership understand how the enterprise is behaving.

The information gathered by cybermonitoring tools includes an indication of the devices that are on the network, the software that is installed on those devices, the ports and protocols that those devices expose on the network, and the data transferred to and from those devices. While network security specialists use this information to identify potential weaknesses in the enterprise's cyberdefenses, it can also be used by enterprise architects to understand the current state of the enterprise. Knowing what software and interfaces are available on the network provides insight into the capabilities available to the enterprise and also identifies facets that can be tested to ensure conformance to enterprise architecture constraints.

In addition to the information available from cybermonitoring tools, most systems generate logs that record which users have accessed a given system, data that has been uploaded or downloaded from that system, and other pertinent factors. This log information can be combined with the information available from cybertools to reveal a great deal of information about the state of the enterprise and the behaviors of the systems and actors within the enterprise. This combined information can be analyzed with a variety of common business intelligence and data analysis tools to generate a near-real-time understanding of the enterprise that is not possible using manual reporting techniques.

# Testing

Traditional enterprise-architecture and system-development techniques begin with a design of the system and create tests that verify the system conforms to the design. These tests are developed in conjunction with the system requirements definition, and are used to verify that the system was built in conformance with the original specification. Additional tests are developed that align with the use cases developed during the construction and design of the system, and these tests are used to validate that the resulting system meets the users' needs. Once a system passes these tests, it is deemed suitable for fielding and put into operation.

This type of development and testing works reasonably well when the development team is using a waterfall development methodology. It even works reasonably well when systems are implemented using Agile development techniques. But as the practice of software development has become increasingly dynamic, this kind of one-and-done testing has become obsolete. Development methodologies such as DevOps have arisen to address the needs of today's dynamic business environment, where capabilities need to evolve in days rather than weeks. Waiting to develop a detailed verification-and-validation plan introduces unacceptable delays that can prevent an enterprise from adapting to changing conditions fast enough to remain competitive.

Replacing an outdated enterprise architecture methodology with a more lightweight and responsive practice will be useless if the enterprise continues to rely on an outdated testing methodology that slows down the enterprise's ability to adapt to changing conditions. Together with a new way of doing enterprise architecture, we must adopt a new way of testing that focuses on enforcing enterprise constraints and ensuring that systems contribute to the enterprise's ability to achieve its goals. Enterprise testing should focus on two things: test-driven development and periodic testing of operational systems.

## Test-Driven Development

Test-driven development is not a new technique, but within the enterprise architecture methodology I am advocating, it becomes a critical component of assessing conformance. The idea of test-driven development is a simple one: give developers the tests that their system must pass before they start development so that they can build the system specifically to pass those tests. Applying this to enterprise architecture means that tests are written to verify conformance to enterprise constraints as the primary means of enforcing those constraints.

It is possible that some systems will not need to conform to some constraints. For example, if you establish a constraint that all systems in the enterprise must encode location information using a degrees-minutes-seconds format, that constraint will not apply to a system that does not deal with location data (such as a payroll system). If your enterprise has a large number of such cases, that may be an indication that the particular constraint is not an appropriate enterprise constraint. But for those cases where you have determined that the enterprise constraint is appropriate, you should take care to plan out how to address those situations where a particular system does not conform to a constraint so that you are not set back when you are managing a large number of system-specific test plans.

The vast majority of constraints will apply to all systems in the enterprise, and so the tests can be established as a minimum procedure that all new system development efforts must pass to ensure conformance with the enterprise architecture. These tests should be automated tests, either executable test harnesses, automated test scripts, or some comparable means of testing that does not require a human to perform the test. The goal is for all systems to use the exact same automated test, as humans might make mistakes or perform the test slightly differently each time, making it difficult to ensure consistency. The goal with test-driven development is to make sure there is no doubt that when tested, the system conforms to the constraints established in the enterprise architecture.

While these tests are provided to developers to ensure that the resulting systems are conformant to enterprise architecture constraints, that is not the only use of the tests. The reality of modern software systems is that they are not static creatures. They are regularly patched and updated to address security vulnerabilities or errors that were not discovered in testing. These changes have a direct effect on the function of the original system. Changes in system configuration settings or the environment in which the system operates may also have an effect on how the system functions. Those effects may impact whether the system still conforms to the constraints of the enterprise architecture. To verify that systems continue to conform to enterprise architecture constraints despite repeated updates, these tests should be run periodically on the fielded systems. You don't want to run them so often that they adversely impact users' ability to employ those systems, but a periodic spot check to verify continued conformance is prudent. This can also be employed to speed up regression testing when a component is updated. Because the enterprise software ecosystem is a complex system, it is difficult to predict all the impacts of upgrading even a single software module, so being able to quickly test the enterprise after an update is a significant risk mitigation.

All systems in the enterprise should conform to the constraints detailed in the enterprise architecture, and that conformance should be verified during the development-and-approval process. However, that does not guarantee that all systems will follow the prescribed course of testing. Every enterprise has systems that slip past the enterprise approval process, operating under the radar as long as they can get away with it. These tools are rarely reported in any manual data call because those who operate and maintain them have a vested interest in keeping them hidden. These systems are deliberately avoiding the enterprise architecture constraints, so there is an excellent chance they are nonconformant. By using cyberscans to identify systems on the network, you eliminate the possibility that such systems will avoid detection. Once detected, they can be tested for conformance to enterprise constraints just as every approved system is, helping to ensure conformance of the entire enterprise.

# Operational Testing

Operational testing has traditionally been the final stage of testing during the system development life cycle. It is particularly common with systems developed for government and military use. During conventional operational testing, the intended users run through a series of scenarios designed to validate system functionality and ensure the system meets the users' needs. Once the system passes operational testing, it is deployed for operational use. This process made sense when systems were developed, deployed, and operated with only infrequent updates that went through the full development-and-testing cycle. The reality of modern code development practices renders this outdated style of operational testing ineffective and ripe for modernization.

In an environment where application code is updated frequently, even multiple times per day in extreme cases, a single operational-testing period makes no more sense than having a doctor treat a patient based on the symptoms experienced the previous week. Just as a patient's condition may worsen or improve over time, the fitness of a given system for its intended use may vary over time. To be effective in today's environment, we must cease viewing operational testing as an event and start looking at it as an ongoing function of system operation and maintenance.

Operational testing is more subjective than conformance testing. While conformance testing is a matter of a system either meeting or failing to meet the defined constraints, operational testing is based on the opinions of human users regarding whether the system being tested meets their needs or not. Opinions will naturally vary from user to user, and may depend somewhat on individual users' abilities and preferences. A tool that is suitable for an expert user may not be usable by a novice, or a tool designed to be user friendly for beginners may make it inconvenient for experienced users to perform complicated tasks.

Whether a system is suitable for a particular need may also depend on the specific circumstances that apply when the system is being used. Environmental factors, available data, mission needs, and many other factors influence whether a system is suitable for the task at hand. These things are all changing constantly, and expecting a system that was well suited for use in one set of circumstances to be suited for use in different circumstances is a very optimistic outlook that is not justified by experience. For example, an e-mail system designed for use on a closed, secure research network with a small user base may not need to defend against things like phishing attacks. But this system may no longer be suitable if the research network is opened up to more users or is connected to the open Internet, where such attacks are common.

Assuming that a system designed for one set of external factors will still be appropriate for a different set of external factors is quite a leap of faith. And while it is possible the system will still be usable to some extent, it is a near certainty that the system will not be nearly as fit for its new purpose as it was for its originally intended purpose. The operational testing that was done at the time the system was originally fielded may no longer reflect the system's usefulness a year later, or even six months later in a very dynamic environment.

For all these reasons, operational testing must be an ongoing process that never truly ends. To some extent, you can gauge a system's operational utility by looking at how often it is used and by whom. It is reasonable to conclude that any system that is used often and by a large community is suitable for some operational tasks and is important to the enterprise. However, the inverse of that statement is not true—the fact that a system is not used often or is used by only a small community does not mean that system is unimportant or not suitable for its tasks. For example, every bank has an alarm system. It would be foolish to conclude that the alarm system is unimportant just because it is rarely used. Judging a system's operational utility by the frequency of use has the advantage of being a nonintrusive means of getting feedback, as you can get this information without having to distract users from their actual work to ask questions about the tools they are using to do that work.

Frequency of use is a reasonable proxy for operational utility, but you should not rely on it as the only measure. There is no substitute for getting feedback from the actual users of the system or capability. It is possible that a system is terrible at performing its intended function, but people use it because it is the only alternative. This is the kind of information that can only be gathered by directly asking the human users. Sometimes, there are no nonintrusive ways to get feedback on the operational utility of a system. Just be mindful of the fact that giving you feedback is not someone's primary job, and time spent providing feedback is time not spent on achieving the enterprise's goals. Keeping your information requests short and to the point is the best way to avoid needless distractions.

Also bear in mind that when you get this feedback, it is important to get feedback from the right set of users. When we think of "users," we generally think of the people who are using the graphical user interface to a system, and we consider it important to get their feedback. But some users are the developers of other systems and capabilities. Consider the case of an enterprise authentication service that developers use to secure the services and capabilities they develop. This authentication service is invisible to most end users; all they see is that they are either able to log in or not. Developers who have to use the interface provided by the authentication service may have a very different opinion of that service's usability and effectiveness.

# Continuous Monitoring

Earlier, I briefly mentioned that most enterprises employ some form of continuous monitoring as part of their cyberdefense plans, and that this monitoring can be leveraged to enable ongoing testing. However, there are many other benefits that the enterprise architect can derive from continuous monitoring and it is useful to discuss them at some length.

For many years, the idea of directly querying every system on the network to discover its capabilities and understand its structure was an unfulfilled dream. The major problem was how to do the scanning. Scanning from a central location has many difficulties that has caused remote monitoring to be rejected in the past: Firewalls block access to systems; systems will only respond to properly formatted requests on ports they are listening on; and any information acquired through a scan looks like a hacking attempt. But the increasing threat of cybercrime has driven a change in how most enterprises operate their networks, and we can take advantage of that change to improve the practice of enterprise architecture.

Most enterprises use cybermonitoring tools that install an agent on each device attached to the network, and that agent gathers information and periodically reports it to a monitoring server. Very large enterprises may have a number of these servers at different locations that roll their information up to a central enterprise server that gives a complete picture of the cybersituation of the enterprise. This information is used by network and system management teams for things like intrusion detection, insider threat detection, and patch management. The same information gathered for use in cyberdefense can be used by enterprise architects to improve the planning and operation of the enterprise's systems.

Before continuing, I would like to add a note of caution based on some painful lessons I have learned. When you ask system or network administrators for access to data from their cybermonitoring tools, you are very likely to meet resistance and skepticism. The data gathered by cybermonitoring agents reveals a great deal about the security measures and vulnerabilities of systems on the network, and that is very sensitive information that network administrators are very reluctant to share. This information could also contain sensitive personal information or company proprietary information that requires careful protection. This is especially true in government settings where interagency rivalries make people leery of revealing any of their shortcomings. I have learned the hard way that asking for cyberdata may generate immediate resistance and an assertion that the requested data is too sensitive to share. It is important that you emphasize that the information you want for enterprise architecture purposes is nonthreat data. For enterprise architecture uses, you really don't care about the vulnerabilities of individual systems or the patch status of specific software. One description of the data that doesn't raise as many concerns is the term *network telemetry data*. This may not be true for all audiences, but these potential sensitivities are something you should keep in mind when requesting access to this data. You are presenting a novel use of cyberdata, and a new concept must be carefully explained to the affected stakeholders. These stakeholders will not only want to understand exactly what data you want from them; they will also want to know what benefit there is for them in sharing the information. In a nutshell, when they ask, "What's in it for me?" you should have a good answer.

There are many possible uses for the data gathered by cybermonitoring agents, and you will no doubt think of many more than I discuss here. But there are four areas that I think are of particular interest to all enterprise architects, and they are worth discussing in brief. They are portfolio management, policy compliance, understanding enterprise capability, and data flow monitoring.

# Portfolio Management

Portfolio management is the ability to understand and make decisions about a set of things you are trying to control. In the case of enterprise architecture, portfolio management is primarily concerned with understanding and optimizing the collection systems used by the enterprise.

The first rule of portfolio management is that you cannot manage what you do not understand. Within a small enterprise, there is a good chance that the chief information officer or other responsible executive will have a good record of what systems are on the network and what software is installed across the enterprise. Many midsized enterprises, and all large enterprises, face a much different situation. An enterprise with multiple business units or cost centers often has many independent system development efforts taking place, with software procurements going on in each unit, and has little central coordination or control. Where enterprises have been grown through merging two or more existing enterprises, this problem is often exacerbated because each of the original enterprises had its own management system and integrating the management systems may be significantly harder than merging the organizations was.

As a result, most large enterprises don't really know what is on their network at the enterprise level. Individual business units may know, and local network administrators probably know as well, but that does not mean the enterprise knows. Capturing that information and reporting it to the enterprise has generally been a manual process, and it is usually seen by local administrators and managers as a distraction from their real work. As a result, when senior leaders ask for information about what systems are operating in the enterprise, the reporting is usually perfunctory and does the minimum needed to answer the questions in the request. More importantly, the information is often inaccurate or out of date, especially if it was derived from the system architecture products. As discussed earlier, architectures never survive first contact with the implementation team, so what is depicted in the architecture may not reflect what is actually operating on the network.

The data gathered by cybermonitoring tools solves this problem very nicely, because instead of relying on outdated design artifacts, it is based on the automated discovery of what is actually on the network. Cybermonitoring tools are usually host based, and will report all the software that is installed on a given host, the version number of that software, the IP address of the host, the ports open on that host, and additional information as configured by the system administrator (usually specified by enterprise policy). Most cybermonitoring capabilities will include some collection of system logs, which gather information about who is using the system, data flowing into and out of the system, and what other systems are connecting to this one. This information provides an up-to-the-minute depiction of what is in the enterprise, what is connected to the network, and how the systems are interacting. Put another way, the tools provide an accurate depiction of the as-is architecture of an enterprise. In many cases, this information can be parsed and loaded into an architecture tool to enable a rapid comparison to the enterprise's reference architecture.

Using cyberinformation to document the enterprise's as-is architecture has two major advantages over issuing a traditional request. First, it doesn't require anyone to create a report to send to senior management. Since the information is already being gathered in a central server, it can be queried without adding to network administrators' workload. Second, the information provided will be current and completely accurate. It is the information being reported by the cyberagents installed on each system. There is no interpretation, no inadvertent omission, and no hiding. It would be naïve to believe that there are no "bootleg" systems in your enterprise—systems that have not been through the standard review and approval process. But these systems exist for a variety of reasons; most of them good. In some cases, they are developed and maintained because enterprise leadership has not responded to the needs of a small but important user community. In other cases, immediate business needs required producing a response faster than the standard review process could support. In the aftermath of the terrorist attacks of September 11, 2001, for instance, a number of intelligence analysis systems were rapidly developed and fielded; the need of the mission was so urgent that the standard review cycle was often waived. Cybermonitoring data will reveal those systems that have not been through the review process, and the outlying systems will reveal to leadership that it has overlooked some important enterprise needs.

Cybermonitoring can also help the portfolio management task by revealing all the software that is deployed across the enterprise. When an enterprise wants to save money by purchasing enterprise licenses for commonly used software, it is important to understand just how commonly used that software is. While buying an enterprise license for a high-profile software package that is only used by a single system with a limited user base may not yield the expected savings, purchasing an enterprise license for a less-well-known software package that is installed across many systems may yield substantial savings. Only when enterprise leadership has visibility into the real state of the enterprise can it make decisions based on facts instead of suppositions.

# Policy Compliance

Ensuring that the enterprise is complying with applicable policy such as laws and regulations, and that systems within the enterprise comply with enterprise policy, is an important activity for any organization. Unfortunately, compliance assessment often requires a labor-intensive manual data collection-and-analysis effort. Some compliance efforts are easy to automate, such as verifying that employees fill out electronic time cards at the end of each day. The payroll system can be configured to automatically check that employees do this. But how do you check whether the payroll system is using the correct virus protection software or is using the enterprise-mandated authentication system?

Your cybermonitoring system is gathering much of the data you need to perform many of these assessments. Assessing whether every system in the enterprise is using the approved version of a software package is an easy task; the cybermonitoring software is likely reporting this information already. But the system is also gathering other information that can be used for more detailed assessments to reveal compliance (or noncompliance) with other aspects of enterprise policy.

Consider a straightforward case wherein the enterprise has a policy that all systems must have public interfaces accessible to other systems within the enterprise. Cyberagents scan each system, and in addition to reporting what software the systems are running, they usually report the ports that have processes listening on them for a connection. Any system in the enterprise that has no open ports obviously does not have a publicly available interface and is therefore noncompliant with the enterprise policy.

Most cases are likely to be less straightforward, and the cyberscanning capability probably won't give definitive answers. But it will give clues that managers can follow up on to verify compliance. More importantly, these clues will be specific, allowing managers to focus on exactly those areas where there may be a problem. One example is interface specification conformance. There are areas where commonality across systems benefits the enterprise by improving the modularity of systems. For example, systems that use geospatial products such as maps often use interfaces that conform to the specifications published by the Open Geospatial Consortium (OGC). By using services that conform to the OGC specifications, systems can use visualization tools from different vendors without having to reengineer the service interfaces on the back-end systems. Trading out one visualization component for another is a matter of configuration, not coding, because all the components use the same interface specification. When the cyberscans reveal an open port on a system that provides geospatial information, you know that is a likely target for periodic testing as previously described. It is probable that the system will have some interfaces that are not intended to be OGC conformant because they have other purposes, but at least now you have a factual basis on which to begin testing.

Another useful indicator is the presence of specific software packages on some systems. In many organizations, especially governments, there is increasing pressure to make data sets more readily available. This is usually done by directing system owners to publish information about their data holdings in a publicly available registry such as Data.gov[1] in the United States or the Open Data Portal in the European Union.[2] But how do you know that all data holdings have been registered? Reviewing the information about what software is installed on every system will provide some clues. If a system is running database software such as Oracle or PostgreSQL, it is reasonable to conclude the system is managing a significant amount of data. If the system has no data holdings in the data registry, that is an indicator that the system should be investigated further to determine whether the data should be registered or not (some databases may be used for purely internal functions such as managing user preferences).

The information provided by the monitoring tools used for cyberdefense will not reveal everything you want to know about systems' compliance with enterprise policy, but it will provide some important clues that will help you focus your efforts. Instead of asking each organization if it's using the enterprise-approved version of a particular software package, you can gather that information from the cybertools and focus your efforts on determining why some programs do not comply and if there is a valid operational reason for that noncompliance.

## Enterprise Capability

As system development and evolution become more dynamic, it is becoming harder for any enterprise to understand the full range of capabilities it really has at its disposal. A system designed to do geospatial analysis might also include a capability suitable for cataloging other types of data. Tools intended for analyzing application logs may also be usable for analyzing text data from other sources. Because systems are usually targeted to a particular use, descriptions of their capabilities tend to be tailored toward the intended user community. Others reading the description may not realize that the

---

[1]You can search the US Government's open data on the Data.gov website at www.data.gov.
[2]The EU Open Data Portal is available at https://data.europa.eu/euodp/en/data/.

system actually has a more generic capability that can be used for "off-label" purposes. An enterprise may not fully appreciate the full set of capabilities available from the tools and systems on hand.

Just as cybermonitoring tools can reveal all the software in use across the enterprise, they can also help reveal the extent of capabilities available to the enterprise. The only catch is that cybermonitoring tools do not track capabilities; they track software and systems. Understanding the capability provided by a system will require some supplementary information.

Fortunately, the needed information should be readily available from the system's architecture documentation. Regardless of the system architecture framework being used, the purpose of the architecture framework is to devise how the resulting system will be constructed to provide some definable capability. Furthermore, the system test plan should identify some specific tasks that the system can perform, as these are the things most in need of testing. By correlating the information gathered from cybermonitoring tools with the system architecture documentation, we can determine what capabilities each system on the network is supposed to provide. This will have the added benefit of revealing duplicate capabilities across the enterprise. For example, comparing the capabilities provided by all the systems in the enterprise may reveal that multiple systems store architecture models. This may verify that the enterprise has an adequate backup and fail-over capability, or it may reveal that the enterprise has an unintended duplicative capability. Regardless of whether the duplication was intended or not, being aware of that duplication is important to effective enterprise management.

By the same token, this assessment of available capabilities can reveal capability gaps in the enterprise. Discovering that there is only one database installed in the enterprise may indicate that there is no database backup or fail-over capability. It is far better to identify such an oversight during an analysis than during a crisis. Alternatively, an enterprise that is trying to improve its customer service might decide to implement a customer resource management system. Before making the decision to procure a new system, the enterprise can identify that it has the ability to capture customer contact information and customer service history, and needs only some basic integration of those two capabilities to meet it customer resource management needs.

To make this comparison practical, the enterprise needs two things: system architectures that are captured as formal models and a controlled vocabulary for describing system capabilities. As discussed earlier, capturing system architectures as formal models makes it easy to compare models to each other and to the enterprise architecture. But this comparison of architecture models will not yield helpful results unless the architectures use the same terms when describing the same capability. This is why including controlled vocabularies in the enterprise architecture, and insisting that system architectures conform to those vocabularies, is so important. Analyzing hundreds of pages of documentation and dozens of models to try to understand a system's capabilities is a time-consuming and error-prone process. The effective use of models and controlled vocabularies makes it easy to automate this process and will greatly reduce the error rate.

## Data Flows

One of the more challenging tasks for any enterprise is to truly understand how data flows through the enterprise, who uses that data, and what the data is used for. This is one of the key areas in which the enterprise will recognize emergent behaviors. Just because data is gathered for a given purpose does not mean the data is not critical to other purposes as well. A prime example is the cybermonitoring data discussed in the previous sections. This data is gathered to improve the enterprise's cybersecurity posture, but, as we have seen, it can also be used to understand and manage the enterprise architecture.

Most systems in an enterprise generate log files that document who logged into the system, what data was uploaded to or downloaded from the system, and similar information. This information can be used to understand how data flows through the enterprise and where it is is used. Seeing how data flows among systems may reveal unanticipated uses of data. For example, consider an enterprise that produces paints and other coatings for outdoor use. It would be natural for such an enterprise to have a weather-monitoring system to help control for variations in temperature and humidity during the manufacturing process. Examining data flows across the enterprise may reveal that the product-ordering system used by customers is retrieving data from the weather system. This may seem like an odd use of weather data, but in investigating it you may learn that the ordering system requires a quasi-random number to be used in the encryption algorithm that keeps customer orders secure, and has determined that using the humidity level recorded by the weather system provides sufficient randomness and saves them the expense of creating a stand-alone random number generator.

While the preceding example is somewhat trivial, it does illustrate the concept that data often has unanticipated uses that benefit the enterprise in unexpected ways. There are other valuable uses of data flow information that we can exploit as well. One example is identifying critical nodes and communications channels in a widely distributed enterprise. Many large enterprises have operations in a large number of widely dispersed locations. Understanding the vulnerabilities in this wide communications network can be difficult. It is a straightforward-enough matter to understand that if the data center hosting the payroll system loses power, the payroll system will go down. But knowing what other systems may be affected is a more difficult question to answer.

By examining the data flows among systems, it is possible to identify potential secondary and tertiary effects of the loss of any single system or communications path. If the payroll system goes down, it is obvious that the payroll system and any other system that connects to that payroll system will be affected. But there may be other systems in the enterprise that do not connect directly to the payroll system but to unaffiliated systems. These are potential secondary impacts of the loss of the payroll system.

When the data flow information from the entire enterprise is collated, it can be loaded into a directed graph. This structure makes it easy to analyze the data flow information and identify the most critical systems (i.e., those with the most connections to other systems) and the most critical communications channels (i.e., those with the most data flowing across them) in the enterprise.

There are many possible uses of data flow information, but there is one additional use that is worth mentioning in specific. Enterprises of all sizes, whether government or private sector, are increasingly aware of the problem posed by the insider threat. High-profile cases of government and corporate espionage have made it clear that identifying trusted actors within the enterprise who may be gathering data for nefarious purposes is a major concern. By capturing the data flow information from system logs over time, you can build up a corpus of information that reflects the normal operation of the enterprise. Which systems normally exchange data with one another? What are the usual volumes of data flow among different systems? Do data flows vary by time of day or in some set pattern? These are all important questions that can reveal the pattern of life of the enterprise. Understanding the standard flow of data across the enterprise makes it possible to identify unusual activity that may be an indicator that something is wrong. Noticing abnormal activity is not definitive proof of a problem; it could just represent unusual business circumstances such as people working overtime to fulfill an unexpected order. But it will at least highlight an area worth investigating and help the enterprise focus resources on those areas.

# Reporting

Gathering information from cybermonitoring tools and system logs is of little use if the information collected cannot be understood and acted upon by enterprise leadership. While many of the senior executives in the enterprise may have an engineering background, their current duties make lengthy explanations of enterprise-monitoring information impractical; they need information summarized in a format that they can both understand and relate to those things they find important—enterprise goals.

Traditionally, status reporting has been document based, focusing on delivering detailed multipage reports or presentations that provide an initial overview of the material followed by more detailed breakdowns. There are two problems with this approach. First, it assumes that the recipient of the report has the time to read it or sit through the presentation. Senior executives are busy, and getting time on their calendar can be difficult. Second, the information is old almost as soon as the report is created. Creating reports takes time, usually a few days to prepare followed by several review cycles. By the time the report reaches the intended audience, it is likely at least two weeks behind. And the more senior the audience, the older and staler the information will be. Making decisions based on outdated information is a terrible way to run an enterprise, especially given the speed of change in today's environments.

A far better way to make this information available to senior leadership is through the use of near-real-time dashboards that display the information. Once the cybermonitoring and system log data has been gathered and collated, the most efficient way to store it is in a database. Once in the database, the information can be queried, analyzed, and displayed in any format that is appropriate to the data and is understandable to the intended decision maker. Furthermore, databases can enforce very fine-grained access controls to ensure that data is not revealed to those who do not have a valid need to access that information.

Dashboards can be created with a number of readily available tools and libraries. Commercial and open-source business intelligence tools can query and analyze data in a wide array of formats and storage schemas. Most such products offer many types of displays, including pie charts, bar graphs, scatterplots, and any number of other similar data visualizations. In addition, highly customized displays can be created using scripting languages such as JavaScript, Python, and Perl, among others.

The important thing about developing dashboard displays is that they must be tailored to the intended use. The best way to do this is to meet with each of the intended users and find out exactly what questions he or she needs answers to on a regular basis.

143

These questions are likely to run the gamut from basic questions such as, "What systems are on the network?" to more sophisticated questions about how many different versions of a particular software package are operating in the enterprise. Once you know the important questions to answer, creating queries that will retrieve that information from the collected data is a straightforward matter.

It will probably take some trial and error to determine what displays work best for each question, and it is possible that different users will want to see the same information presented in different displays. In reality, there is no easy way to solve this problem other than to create some candidate displays and get the users' feedback. Asking each user how he or she wants to see a given data set displayed is often frustrating. Many users cannot tell you what they want in terms of a data display, but they will certainly be able to tell you what they do not like. Showing them candidate displays is an excellent way to get useful feedback on what displays will be helpful to each user.

An additional benefit of using live displays instead of static reports is that users can interact with the information. Most business intelligence tools include the ability to drill down into data to see the details behind a given visualization. Depending on the nature of the specific data used for a given visualization and how it is stored, it may be an easy thing to show other data that is related to that shown in the first display. For example, if the data is stored using a graph data structure such as resource description framework or a property graph, then displaying the underlying graph and allowing users to navigate from one node to another to see the relationships among the data elements will be easy.

Ultimately, your reporting methodology must meet the needs of the intended users and must answer their important questions. It is a safe bet that these questions will be directly related to understanding how the enterprise is progressing toward its goals, and so starting with displays related to those goals is a good plan.

# Summary

Measuring the effects that result from the emergent behaviors of the enterprise is the ultimate means of determining if the enterprise is making progress toward the goals that were defined at the beginning of the enterprise architecture effort. It is basic human nature that we pay attention to those things we are being graded on, and so people will pay the most attention to those aspects of the enterprise that are being measured and reported to senior management.

Testing has been a part of system development since systems were first developed, but the traditional method of testing after system implementation and integration assumes that there is a single implementation-and-integration cycle. Development methodologies such as Agile and DevOps deliver new products every couple of weeks or more often, and testing is a nearly continuous activity. Continuing to treat testing as a one-time event that occurs at the end of the development cycle is an outdated way of approaching testing.

Modern enterprises should approach system testing as the starting point of the development cycle, focusing on defining those tests that judge how a system fits into the overall enterprise. This means focusing on interface testing—the details of internal functioning are outside the scope of the enterprise architecture. By starting with interface tests and employing a test-driven development strategy, the enterprise architecture team can focus on driving interoperability where it matters most and leave the implementation details to the implementation teams. These interface tests need to be rerun periodically to ensure that systems continue to conform to them as the systems evolve.

Operational testing has also been seen as something that happens once at the end of the development cycle. This validation step is usually seen as the final approval before a system is released for widespread use. But in an environment where business needs change and new behaviors emerge constantly, operational testing needs to be a continuous process that ensures a given system or capability continues to be usable for its intended purpose. Assuming that a system is just as useful five years after it was developed is optimistic to say the least.

Constant testing and assessment would be a labor-intensive process if undertaken using traditional testing methods. Moreover, capturing and understanding the emergent behaviors of the enterprise would be even more labor intensive due to the difficulty of understanding how users interact with systems and how systems interact with one another. The cybermonitoring tools used in most enterprises gather a wide variety of data that can be used to understand these emergent behaviors and how the enterprise is progressing toward achieving its goals without imposing any additional burdens that distract staff from their normal tasks.

One immediate benefit that cybermonitoring tools can provide is in the area of portfolio management. In many large enterprises, it is an unfortunate fact of life that no one really knows what systems are on the network or how those systems relate to one another. Cybermonitoring tools are already gathering that information, but most enterprises are not using it to help understand their as-is enterprise architecture.

Verifying policy compliance is another area where cybermonitoring tools can be used by the enterprise architecture team to understand the state of the enterprise and guide it toward meeting enterprise goals. Cybermonitoring tools usually do some measure of policy compliance verification, but it is usually focused on things like ensuring that systems are patched up to prescribed levels. The data gathered by cybermonitoring tools may not reveal the full extent of how well individual systems are complying with enterprise policy, but they can reveal clues that will help the enterprise architecture team focus its efforts on the areas that are most likely to need attention.

Cybermonitoring tools will also help enterprise leadership understand the variety of capabilities available across the enterprise. By revealing the truth about which hosts and software are operating on the network, cybermonitoring tools make it possible to understand all the capabilities available in the enterprise and not just those that are directly supervised at the enterprise level.

One of the most important things the enterprise architecture team can monitor is the flow of data into, out of, and through the enterprise. This information is usually available from a combination of cybermonitoring tools and system logs. It will reveal not only where information flows between two systems but which systems and communication channels are the most critical in the enterprise. This information can also reveal potential second- and third-order effects that would result from the loss of any given system or communication channel in the enterprise—conclusions difficult to draw through reviewing architecture documents.

Finally, all this information must be made available to senior leadership in a readily understandable format that is updated in near real time. Stale information is a poor source for making decisions, and combing the information available from cybermonitoring tools with the analysis tools and visualizations available from commercial or open-source business intelligence tools makes creating user-friendly, up-to-date data displays easier than producing traditional paper reports or presentations. The kind of data visibility such tools provide is key to helping senior leadership understand the current state of the enterprise and its progress toward achieving its goals.

# APPENDIX A

# References

The following works are nowhere near all that has been written on each of these subjects, but they do provide useful background material to the contents of this book.

You can also check out my blog at `http://jmcdowall.org/` for more information on the subjects. While I was working on my doctorate, I kept an online dissertation journal to help me keep track of my progress and keep a running tally of relevant topics in a place where I couldn't lose them. After finishing up this book, I've had a lot of related but off-topic thoughts on how we do system architecture, so I've recently restarted that online journal to keep track of these ideas.

## Enterprise Architecture Frameworks

"DODAF: DOD Architecture Framework Version 2.02: DOD Deputy Chief Information Officer." US Department of Defense: Chief Information Officer. Accessed November 12, 2018. `https://dodcio.defense.gov/Library/DoD-Architecture-Framework/dodaf20_background/`.

Open Group. *TOGAF*, version 9. Open Group. Last modified February 2, 2009. `https://publications.opengroup.org/g091`.

Zachman, J. A. "A Framework for Information Systems Architecture." *IBM Systems Journal* 26, no. 3 (1987): 276–92.

## Enterprise Architecture Practice

Bloomberg, Jason. "Is Enterprise Architecture Completely Broken?" *Forbes*. Last modified July 11, 2014. `www.forbes.com/sites/jasonbloomberg/2014/07/11/is-enterprise-architecture-completely-broken/`.

© John D. McDowall 2019
J. D. McDowall, *Complex Enterprise Architecture*, https://doi.org/10.1007/978-1-4842-4306-0

Dang, Dinh Duong, and Samuli Pekkola. "Problems of Enterprise Architecture Adoption in the Public Sector: Root Causes and Some Solutions." In *Information Technology Governance in Public Organizations: Theory and Practice*, edited by Lazar Rusu and Gianluigi Viscusi, 177–98. Integrated Series in Information Systems 38. Cham, Switzerland: Springer International Publishing, 2017.

Hadar, Ethan, and Gabriel M. Silberman. "Agile Architecture Methodology: Long Term Strategy Interleaved with Short Term Tactics." In *Companion to the 23rd ACM SIGPLAN Conference on Object-Oriented Programming Systems Languages and Applications*, 641–52. New York: ACM, 2008. https://dl.acm.org/citation.cfm?doid=1449814.1449816.

Welke, MaryAnn. "The Death of Enterprise Architecture?" LinkedIn. July 28, 2017. www.linkedin.com/pulse/death-enterprise-architecture-maryann-welke/.

# Modeling Languages

"About the Business Process Model and Notation Specification Version 2.0." Object Management Group. January 2011. www.omg.org/spec/BPMN/2.0/.

Friedenthal, Sanford, Alan Moore, and Rick Steiner. *A Practical Guide to SysML: The Systems Modeling Language.* (3rd ed.) Waltham, MA: Morgan Kaufmann, 2014.

Jaakkola, Hannu, and Bernhard Thalheim. "Architecture-Driven Modelling Methodologies." In *Information Modelling and Knowledge Bases XXII, 20th European-Japanese Conference on Information Modelling and Knowledge Bases (EJC 2010)*, 97–116, Amsterdam, NL: IOS Press, 2010. https://www.researchgate.net/publication/221014046_Architecture-Driven_Modelling_Methodologies.

Rumbaugh, James, Ivar Jacobson, and Grady Booch. *The Unified Modeling Language Reference Manual*, 2nd ed. Boston, MA: Pearson Higher Education, 2004.

# Complex Systems/Emergent Behaviors

Epstein, Joshua M., and Robert Axtell. *Growing Artificial Societies: Social Science from the Bottom Up.* Washington, DC: Brookings Institution Press, 1996.

Hofstadter, Douglas R. *Gödel, Escher, Bach: An Eternal Golden Braid* (20th Anniversary ed.). New York: Basic Books, 1999.

Holland, John H. "Complex Adaptive Systems." *Daedalus* 121, no. 1 (1992): 17–30.

Mina, Ali A., Dan Braha, and Yaneer Bar-Yam. "Complex Engineered Systems: A New Paradigm." In *Complex Engineered Systems: Science Meets Technology*, edited by Dan Braha, Ali A. Minai, and Yaneer Bar-Yam, 1–21. Berlin: Springer, 2006.

# Miscellaneous

E. W. Dijkstra, "A Note on Two Problems in Connexion with Graphs," *Numerische Mathematik* 1, no. 1 (December 1, 1959): pp. 269–271.

# Index

## A

Actors, 45–46, 72–73
    data, 73–74
    modeling data, 75–76
      object data, 77–78
      tuple data, 76–77
    syntax and semantics, 74–75
Adaptive systems and
      enterprise architecture, 20–21
    constraints, 27–29
    emergent behaviors, 30–33
    goals, 21–23
    rules, 24–27
Agent-based software
      systems, 16
Agile development techniques, 130
Application log and system log
      analysis tools, 111
Architecture frameworks, origin
    agile methodology, 6
    DevOps, 6
    heritage, 4
    information systems, 6–7
    software development, 5
    TOGAF model, 4
    Zachman framework, 4
Architecture tool, 11
Association for Computing
      Machinery (ACM), 54
Automated metrics, gathering, 128

## B

Behavior models
    capturing
      application and system logs, 85
      human nature, 84
      interviews or surveys, 84
      personal interviews, 84–85
    characteristics, 82
    documenting
      formalization tool, 86
      time stamps, 87
    enterprise goals, 83
    example, 82, 87–88
    iterative process, 82
    system architecture, 83
Binary Large Object (BLOB), 77
Business goals, 59
Business Process Model and
      Notation (BPMN), 68, 117–118

## C

Capability Maturity Model
      Integration (CMMI), 71
Card validation function, 93
Change control
    change management process, 123
    modeling tools, 122
    version control system, 122
    written record, 123

151

© John D. McDowall 2019
J. D. McDowall, *Complex Enterprise Architecture*, https://doi.org/10.1007/978-1-4842-4306-0

Character Large Object (CLOB), 77
Cloud computing, 89
Color-coding system, 83
Complex adaptive system, 9
    definition, 13
    examples, 14–16
Component systems
    advantages, 96
    enterprise architect, 95
    enterprise-level visibility, 96
    rule of thumb, 95
Conformance testing, 132
Continuous monitoring
    cybermonitoring tools, 135
    data flows, 141–142
    enterprise capability
        controlled vocabulary, 140
        cybermonitoring tools, 140
        error rate, 141
        system's architecture
          documentation, 140
    policy compliance, 138
        cyberdefense, 139
        cybermonitoring system, 138
        cyberscanning, 138
        payroll system, 138
        software packages, 139
    portfolio management, 136–137
    scanning, 134
Cybercriminals, 129
Cybermonitoring, 111, 113, 129, 135–136,
    140, 145–146
Cybersecurity, 84

**D**

Dashboards, 143
Data Definition Language (DDL), 76

Data flows, continuous monitoring
    abnormal activity, 142
    capturing, 142
    cybermonitoring data, 141
    log files, 141
    payroll system, 142
    product-ordering system, 141
De Facto standards
    information technology, 99
    Microsoft word document format, 99
    RFC, 100
De Jure standards
    governments, 98
    military operations, 99
    span functions, 98
    XSD, 98
Department of Defense Architecture
    Framework (DoDAF), 2
Development operations (DevOps), 6, 130
Dynamic enterprise architecture
    agile, 105
    by detail (*see* Dynamic enterprise
      architecture, by detail)
    development team, 105
    DevOps, 105
    management tool, 105
    modern enterprise, 104
    by time (*see* Dynamic enterprise
      architecture, by time)
Dynamic enterprise architecture, by detail
    defining enterprise, 106–107
    reference architecture, 107–108
    scope, 106
    solution architecture, 108–109
Dynamic enterprise architecture, by time
    architecture artifact, 110
    as-is architecture, 110–111
    to-be architecture, 111–112

# E, F

Economics and enterprise
    architecture, 18–19
Emergent behavior, 13
Enterprise architecture
    broken
        business managers, 2
        review, history, 3
    enabling agility, 8–9
    framework
        description of, 38–41
        example of, 37–38
        primary objects (*see* Primary
          objects)
        secondary objects (*see* Secondary
          objects)
    goals, 7
    guiding, 9–11
    system architectures, 11–12
    testing, 130–131, 133–134
Extensible Markup Language (XML), 75

# G, H

General Motors, 106–107

# I

Information systems, 1, 3
Infrastructure environment
    cloud service providers, 89
    communications
        bandwidth, 90
    constraints, 90
    data center, 89
Institute of Electrical and Electronics
    Engineers (IEEE), 54
Intrusion detection, 135

# J, K, L

Joint Photographic Experts
    Group (JPEG), 77
Joint Requirements Oversight Council
    (JROC) process, 27

# M

Machine learning, 104
Mission-type orders, 22
Model-based systems engineering
    (MBSE), 116
Modeling languages
    BPMN, 117–118
    computer program, 115
    OWL, 118–119
    SysML, 116–117
    UML, 115–116
Models creation, enterprise architecture
    architect, 112
    behavior models, 114
    dividing, architecture, 121
    external organizations, 113
    groups of models, 121
    logical components, 122
    modeling language (*see* Modeling
      languages)
    modeling tools, 119
    XMI, 120
Monitoring system, 127
Monolithic systems
    architects, 95
    commercial software, 94
    enterprise architect, 94–95

# N

Network telemetry data, 135

# O

Object data, 77
Object Management Group (OMG), 115
Operational testing
    external factors, 133
    feedback, 134
    frequency of use, 134
    ongoing function, 132
Organizational environment
    enterprise's ability, 91
    external organization, 91
OWL model, 128

# P, Q

Payroll management system, 107
Physical Exchange Specification (PES), 120
Portable Network Graphics (PNG), 77
Portfolio management
    cyberinformation, 137
    cybermonitoring tools, 136
    large enterprises, 136
    small enterprise, 136
    software package, 137
Primary objects
    actors (*see* Actors)
    data, 47–48
    goals, 41, 58–59
        architecture goals, 43–44, 61–64
        enterprise goals, 42–43, 59–61
    processes, 46, 66–67
    processes example, 67–70
    required processes, 70–71
    strategies, 44–45, 64–66

# R

Request for Comment (RFC), 100

# S

Secondary objects
    behavior (*see* Behavior models)
    component systems, 95–96
    environment, 52–53, 88–91, 93
    monolithic systems, 94–95
    standards, 53–55
    systems, 49–50
Solution architectures, 11
Standards, secondary object
    data formats, 97
    de facto, 99–100
    de jure, 98–99
    main forms, 97
Status reporting
    dashboards, 143
    live displays, 144
    senior leadership, 143
    software package, 144
    trial and error, 144
Structured Query Language (SQL), 76
Sugarscape model, 17–18
Swim lanes, 69
System environment
    credit card transaction processor, 93
    external systems, 92–93
    interface, 93
    internal systems, 92
Systems Modeling Language (SysML), 11,
        38, 116–117

# T

Technical Architecture Framework for
        Information Management
        (TAFIM), 4
Test-driven development
    automated, 131

constraints, 131

cyberscans, 132

goal, 131

software ecosystem, 131

The Open Group Architecture Framework
        (TOGAF), 2, 4

Traditional enterprise architecture
        frameworks, 20, 94, 103, 105, 109

Transport Layer
        Security (TLS), 25

Tuple data, 76

## U

Unified Modeling Language (UML), 23,
        25, 38, 115–116

## V

Version control system, 122

Visio, 11

## W

Web Ontology Language
        (OWL), 77, 118–119

## X, Y

XML Schema Definition (XSD), 76, 98

## Z

Zachman framework, 4–5

Printed in Great
Britain
by Amazon

31371946R00099